ENABLING
ROMANCE

ENABLING ROMANCE

A Guide to Love, Sex, and Relationships for the Disabled

(AND THE PEOPLE WHO CARE ABOUT THEM)

ERICA KLEIN & KEN KROLL

Harmony Books

Published by Harmony Books, a division of Crown Publishers, Inc., 201 East 50th Street, New York, New York 10022. Member of the Crown Publishing Group.

HARMONY and colophon are trademarks of Crown Publishers, Inc.

Manufactured in the United States of America

Library of Congress Cataloging-in-Publication Data
Kroll, Ken.
    Enabling romance: a guide to love, sex, and relationships for the disabled (and the people who care about them) / by Ken Kroll and Erica Levy Klein; with illustrations by Mark Langeneckert.
    Includes bibliographical references.
    1. Sex instruction for the physically handicapped. 2. Physically handicapped—Sexual behavior. 3. Interpersonal relations.
I. Klein, Erica Levy. II. Title.
HQ54.2.K76 1992
613.9'6'087—dc20   91-20560
                CIP

ISBN 0-517-57532-9
10 9 8 7 6 5 4 3 2 1
FIRST EDITION

FOR OUR THREE JEWISH MOTHERS,

Victoria Kroll,
Mildred Levy,
and Susanna Bensinger

Contents

Contents

Acknowledgments

The authors gratefully acknowledge the following for permission to reprint previously copyrighted material:

Harper & Row for excerpts from *Comeback: Six Remarkable People Who Triumphed over Disability* by Frank Bowe, 1981.

Association Press for excerpts from *The Sexually Oppressed*, edited by Harvey and Jean Gochros, 1977.

A WORD ABOUT LANGUAGE —AND A WORD OR TWO ABOUT RESEARCH

anguage is a key issue in the disability rights movement. It plays an important role because language has traditionally been used as a way to quickly label and stigmatize people with disabilities and separate them from the rest of the population. Words like *crippled* and *deformed* and phrases like *suffer from* and *victim of* all suggest someone who is pitiful and helpless rather than a viable human being who deserves to be treated just like everyone else.

Today there is growing awareness of how language can create either a straightforward, positive impression of people with disabilities or an insensitive portrayal that reinforces common myths and is just another form of discrimination. In most cases while writing *Enabling Romance*, we used the preferred terminology outlined by the National Institute on Disability and Rehabilitation Research in "Guidelines for Reporting and Writing About People with Disabilities," such as *people with disabilities* rather than the often-used term *the handicapped*. Although opinions may differ on some of these terms, these guidelines represent the current consensus about acceptable terms among the nation's leading disability organizations.

Our only point of departure from the guidelines is in our use of the word *disabled* as a modifier or as a collective noun, as in "disabled person" and "the disabled." Although we strongly support focusing on the person first and not the disability, we feel that neither term implies any negative value judgment, nor does it lump people with disabilities together, but simply represents an alternative way of referring to "people with disabilities" without constantly resorting to verbal gymnastics. In an atmosphere where language has historically been used as a tool of oppression, it is understandable that all language referring to disabilities should undergo close scrutiny, but we feel that never being able to say "the disabled" or refer to "a disabled person" is overly sensitive and unnecessary.

We relied on hundreds of questionnaires mailed to people with disabilities and to those with disabled partners to provide the true-life experiences that are the heart and soul of this book. Over the course of a year's research, more than seventy-five individuals and couples took the time to share with us their most intimate experiences and to give us greater insight into what it's like to be a social, romantic, and sexual being who also happens to have a disability.

The truth is that the people who responded to our questionnaire are just as much the authors of this book as we are. It is their words and thoughts that we hope will give *Enabling Romance* its power to reach others with disabilities and those who play important roles in their lives. That includes (but by no means is limited to) friends, lovers, spouses, family members, independent living counselors, rehabilitation professionals, nursing home and institutional administrators, personal care attendants, teachers, physicians, health-care workers, and legislators.

One brief aside. Although all the individuals and couples who responded to the questionnaires were heterosexual, we strongly support homosexuality and bisexuality as life-styles that deserve the same respect given to heterosexuality. One in twenty adults is homosexual or bisexual, and this obviously includes many men and women with disabilities. A group called Able Together (P.O. Box 931028, Los Angeles, CA 90093), as well as the National Gay Task Force in New York, can provide information to disabled gays and lesbians about local groups and resources that may be of interest to them.

To all the respondents and professionals who helped us so much, we offer our heartfelt gratitude. We'd like to extend our special thanks to Sandi Gordon, vice president of communications for the National Easter Seal Society of Chicago, who helped us distribute our questionnaire to Easter Seal chapters across the country; Stanley Ducharme, director of the Sexuality and Disability Center of Boston University Medical Center, for his conscientious review and critique of our initial manuscript; and the publishers and staffs of *Accent on Living* magazine, *The Disability Rag, Independent Living,* and *Spinal Network Extra* for additional input and advice as well as for their pioneering efforts in disability awareness and civil rights. A special thank-you goes to Michael Hall of the Lawrence Research Group, publisher of the Xandria Collection catalog, which issues a separate edition featuring sexual aids specially modified for people with disabilities.

In the chapters that follow, you'll become more familiar with the lives of many people with disabilities, both individuals and couples, including the story of how we got to know each other, fell in love, and became husband and wife. Although all the stories are real, some of the information may have been edited or expanded for clarity, and occasionally—when we were reasonably certain about the facts of someone's life but could not track them down because many years had passed— we developed their stories strictly from memory.

We deliberately chose not to censor individual accounts, even when they contained self-deprecating, out-of-date, or slang terms for disabilities or sexual acts. People speak with many voices, and we feel that it is important to respect this diversity of expression.

You may also notice that many people are referred to by their first names. To protect the identities of those respondents who elected to remain anonymous, these may or may not be the actual first names of the individuals who answered our questionnaire.

We hope you will enjoy reading *Enabling Romance* as much as we've enjoyed writing it. We welcome your comments and invite you or your organization to contact us in care of our publisher:

—Ken Kroll and Erica Levy Klein c/o Harmony Books
Crown Publishing Group
201 East Fiftieth St.
New York, NY 10022

$\boxed{\textit{Part One}}$

THE FINAL TABOO: SEXUAL SATISFACTION FOR PEOPLE WITH DISABILITIES

Chapter 1

OUR OWN LOVE STORY: HOW THE AUTHORS GOT TOGETHER

Ken

Despite the admittedly dark realities that often face people with disabilities, this book is bright testimony to the love of two people, one disabled, the other not. It was inspired when we discovered that, in spite of our deep appreciation for each other, we were both having a difficult time understanding each other's worlds. I found it hard to accept the fact that nondisabled people like my fiancée (and now wife), Erica Levy Klein, viewed me as "different," someone to be approached tentatively and treated gingerly. And she sometimes found it equally hard to accept that people stared at us wherever we went and regarded us as part novelty, part aberration.

Looking back, I can see that the issues this book raises about social and sexual equality were present in our own relationship right from the morning of our first date.

I had hoped that an elegant breakfast at a posh hotel would set the right tone for a relaxed first get-together. And that's exactly what it turned out to be—relaxed and uncomplicated. We sat in the near-empty dining room the day after Christmas, laughing and talking like old friends. For a while we pretended to study the menu, ignoring the young, tuxedoed waiter who hovered expectantly, waiting to take our orders.

I can't remember how much time passed until it occurred to us that it was all right to eat breakfast on a breakfast date. Maybe it was a hour, maybe two. All I remember is that it was gray and cold outside, but inside that dining room I was basking in sunshine. I was finally face to face with this terrific woman I'd met through—of all things—a personals ad in the newspaper.

I had spoken to her only once before. But that was a marathon two-hour phone conversation. We'd talked a lot then, so we already knew a great deal about each other. Even over the phone, she had rekindled my hope that despite two divorces there was still the chance I could experience the lasting happiness that had always eluded me.

Finally, we couldn't keep the waiter at bay any longer. Demonstrating what I was sure was my tremendous savoir faire, I motioned him over and started giving him our order. He looked at me quizzically, then his gaze seemed to lock on my mouth struggling to form the words and the wheelchair I was sitting in.

"What did you say?" he asked as he leaned forward, his face tense and concerned. I repeated my order, but his face was a study in bewilderment.

Erica sensed both the waiter's and my predicament and came to the rescue with her order. "I'll have a croissant, fresh strawberries, and decaf coffee," she said pleasantly.

Relieved, the waiter scribbled down her order. Then, as he turned back to me once again, I pretended to scan the menu one last time. Actually, over the top of the menu, I was watching her eyes. She looked up at me and smiled. I remember it was the first time I felt that I could look into those eyes forever.

"And what will the gentleman have, madame?" the waiter asked, turning to Erica for my order. It was as if I had totally ceased to exist.

Oh, God, I thought, that's it. It's all over now. Now she knows what it's like to be with someone who everyone treats like they're part of the wallpaper. Dammit, I said to myself, she'll probably never go out with me again.

Instead she simply cleared her throat and said firmly, with just a trace of a smile, "I really don't know. You probably ought to ask him." The waiter reddened, reluctantly turning to me.

"I'll make it easy for you"—you bozo, I thought—"I'll have the same."

"Thank you, sir," he said, his smile forced. He hurried back to the kitchen, clearly pleased that the entire episode was over.

After the waiter had gone, there was a lengthy silence.

"Does that happen all the time?" Erica finally asked. "He didn't seem to want to talk to you."

"I'm afraid so," I replied. "I don't think he was purposely being rude. It's just that most people are so unaccustomed to dealing with someone with a disability, they just freeze up. And if the disabled person is with someone who's not disabled, they think they've got an easy way out."

"Hey," she said throwing her head back and laughing, "who ever said I was easy?"

Thank God she's laughing, I thought. At least she isn't getting up and walking out.

"It's hard to believe this kind of thing really happens," she continued, "but I guess it just did."

"And it probably will again and again," I explained. "It's

just something you get used to."

Here we were on our first date, and all I was doing was explaining how the world reacts to my disability. Fortunately, Erica realized I wanted to change the subject. "So, how about telling me your life story," she suggested. "In twenty-five words or less, of course," she said, grinning.

That's when I relaxed and told her everything. How I'd been married twice before, both times to disabled women, and how my last marriage had been a total disaster that left me extremely reluctant to get involved with anyone again. But how I still longed to find the right person to love, and to love me.

We lingered over coffee, talking about anything and everything. Our lives, our careers, even our past relationships.

It was amazing how much we had in common. Like me, Erica was an advertising copywriter. But, unlike me, she was also an aspiring screenwriter struggling to get her scripts sold and produced, and a travel writer who spent her vacations researching and developing articles. She also did free-lance copywriting on the side—to fill up her spare time, I mused.

What we didn't have in common was her passion for culture and my love of the outdoors. Her idea of roughing it was staying at a Holiday Inn. But, then again, my idea of high culture was playing elevator music on my car stereo.

There were all those small differences to contend with, plus one major one: the undeniable fact that I was disabled and she wasn't.

Later we drove back to her apartment, where we talked for a while before I had to leave on a business trip. Finally it was time to go, and I knew I was about to find out whether she wanted ever to see me again. I'll never forget Erica standing directly in front of my wheelchair and asking me the most welcome question I think I've probably ever heard.

"Do you think you might like a hello hug instead of a good-bye hug?"

Unsteadily, I got out of my wheelchair and took her into

my arms. "Let's give this relationship a try, okay?" I whispered to her as I held her.

"Okay," she said, looking up. "Let's see what happens." Seventeen months later, that "okay" turned into "I do," and the woman I took to breakfast that day became my wife.

Erica

I can still remember how lovely and romantic our first few months together were. But what I remember even more vividly is that for the first time in my life I had to face the fact that people with disabilities are treated completely differently than everybody else. Worst of all, they are often treated as "nonpeople" who don't deserve to be acknowledged; they are simply invisible.

I also had to face the fact that throughout my life I had remained purposely unaware of people with disabilities. My mother had raised me to "stay away from damaged goods" and not to "put a healthy body in a sick bed." In other words, I was to date only perfect people with no problems—not any obvious physical ones, anyway. Even on our first date, I remember asking Ken if his marriage had ended because he wasn't able to have sex. I just naturally assumed that, because he was disabled, sex was a physical impossibility. I was like so many people in that respect; I simply couldn't imagine it.

Naturally, as Ken and I got to know each other better and began an intimate relationship, my awareness level changed. But I think I only realized how much I'd changed when I walked into a local bookstore one day and asked the sales assistant whether they had any books about disabled people and romantic relationships. "Why would anyone want to read a book about *that?*" he said, his face clearly showing his disdain.

And in that moment—in that moment of disbelief—this book was born.

I don't want to give you the impression that everything

was rosy as our relationship progressed from love to marriage. It definitely wasn't. Along the way we struggled, and still struggle, to bridge the gulf that lies between us—the chasm between people with disabilities and those who have never known that experience firsthand. We also experienced the growing pains shared by many of the couples in this book and wondered what role, if any, Ken's disability played in them or if they were simply cases of our different personalities clashing despite our best efforts to mesh them. What we inevitably discovered is that a disability plays a relatively minor role in most relationships once the couple has decided they genuinely want to be together. As with most intimate relationships, it is the strengths and weaknesses of the people involved—not the superficialities—that determine success.

I'm happy to say that once we accepted each other for who we were, and I came to terms with what being involved with Ken would mean, our relationship progressed relatively smoothly. What proved especially difficult for me—apart from the stares and whispers wherever we went—was having to contend with the various friends, family members, and colleagues who offered their well-meaning but unsolicited advice:

He'll always hold you back, Erica. Get out of it now, while you still can.

Wouldn't you rather stick to disabled women, Ken? Don't they understand you better?

C'mon, Erica. You don't need someone like that in your life just when things are beginning to happen for you.

You're out of your league, Ken. She'll dump you in six months.

You can't be serious, Erica! What if his condition gets worse and he turns into a vegetable? (To which I replied through clenched teeth, "Then I'll just have to throw some butter and garlic on him and sauté him.")

That we got married after being on the receiving end of advice like that is nothing short of a miracle. But the comments we heard weren't all that surprising. They reflect society's deeply rooted prejudices and the mistaken belief that people with disabilities simply aren't capable of being full participants in intimate relationships.

Of course, nothing could be further from the truth. What I have learned from knowing Ken is that regardless of a person's physical limitations, and regardless of how his or her outward appearance is affected, the ability to love and be loved remains unaffected. Nor does a disability in any way lessen a person's need for all the things the rest of us seek, including social interaction, romantic involvement, and sexual fulfillment. All human beings are born with the desire for a meaningful connection with others, and not even the most profound disability will change that. I'm a little embarrassed to admit that it took me more than thirty years to figure out something that is so fundamental, so completely obvious. But, happily for me, it was a case of "Better late than never."

Chapter 2

NEUTERED NO MORE: SHATTERING SEXUAL STEREOTYPES

*A*lthough more than 37 million people with disabilities are currently living in the United States and Congress has recently passed sweeping disability rights legislation, the right to sexual expression and satisfaction for disabled people remains the last taboo, the last frontier on the long road to equality.

No one knows exactly how widespread erroneous beliefs about the sexlessness of disabled people are, but Diane Piastro, who writes the nationally syndicated column "Living with a Disability," receives dozens of letters annually from nondisabled readers asking whether sex in any form is possible for someone who is disabled. Although more positive, erotically charged images of disabled people have recently been seen in movies like *Coming Home*, *My Left Foot*, and *Born on the Fourth of*

Enabling Romance

July, society still tends to segregate disabled people and deny their right to participate fully in social, romantic, and sexual relationships. This contributes to widespread lack of understanding about disabilities—especially as they pertain to sexuality and sexual expression. As Piastro writes:

> One of the most common misconceptions about people with disabilities is that they can't have sex, don't want sex or are not interested in sex. People seem to think a disability neuters you sexually. This attitude can be found even among professionals who work with disabled people. Unfortunately, the way people are perceived often becomes the way they perceive themselves.

Gary, a 55-year-old high school principal with quadriplegia, illustrates how even knowledgeable professionals can unwittingly perpetuate damaging myths about disabilities and sexuality.

Gary became a quadriplegic in his twenties, when a powerful wave caught him from behind and hurled him face down into some rocks while he was swimming with several army friends. Gary says he can still recall the strange sensation as a loud snap meant his neck had broken at the sixth cervical vertebra.

A specialist in spinal cord injuries at the VA hospital where Gary was diagnosed told him he could expect to be permanently paralyzed from the neck down. However, after several months of traction and rehabilitative therapy, Gary discovered he could still move his arms (although his hands were almost useless), and he had nearly full sensation in his shoulders and chest to the level of his nipples. He also learned he had limited movement in one leg.

After another six months of intensive physical and occupational therapy, Gary began using a wheelchair, caring for his own basic needs, and driving a car equipped with special controls. He was relieved to be independent once more, but saddened by what he felt were his bleak prospects for ever again having a romantic or sexual relationship.

Every time he asked his doctor what his disability would still allow him to do sexually, Gary was told he had to be realistic. "Just put the whole thing behind you and don't look back," the doctor advised.

Yet, when Gary met Beverly, he began to question that advice. It helped that they were intensely physically attracted to each other from the start. Although Beverly knew Gary's doctors had told him he would never be able to functional sexually again, the chemistry between them was undeniable. And, much to Gary's delight, he found that, despite his being paralyzed, his relationship with Beverly awakened feelings of sexual excitement he never thought he'd experience again.

Slowly, as Gary and Beverly became more intimate, Gary found that he could still experience some feelings of sexual arousal. He was able to redirect these sensations to areas that were not completely paralyzed. His shoulders and chest had become much more erogenous, for example. And, although he couldn't achieve a complete erection, he found he could enjoy the deep pleasure of sexual satisfaction. The sights, sounds, and smells of sex, coupled with Beverly's stimulation of his new erogenous zones, encouraged them both to redefine the way Gary experienced sex. As the months passed, Gary and Beverly found that, with extended periods of tender foreplay, Gary could become partially erect and at times even ejaculate.

Needless to say, Gary no longer accepts verbatim everything he hears. "For a guy they gave up on years ago, I think I'm doing pretty well."

Beverly agrees. "Even after thirty years of marriage, he's still the sexiest man I've ever known," she says with a twinkle in her eye.

The story of Anne, a woman with paraplegia as the result of a skiing accident, strongly resembles Gary's in terms of misguided advice. Anne remembers receiving clear-cut negative messages about sexuality after she was diagnosed:

> *Right after my accident, I asked my doctor if I could still have sex and get pregnant. Those issues were very important to me and to my self-esteem. His reply was something like "No need to worry yourself about those things," which I then interpreted to mean that, since I was disabled, I might as well forget about sex, romance, or anything like that. I became incredibly depressed and felt like my life was over. My mother made things even worse. She considered me her "poor, crippled daughter," and every time I would bring up men she'd change the subject. Disabled people need to have it reaffirmed to them that they can still function sexually and still be complete human beings.*

Jay's experience also testifies to the lack of training about sexuality among many rehabilitation professionals. Jay is a professional writer who lost both legs above the knee when his single-engine plane crashed. For a while he had significant problems adjusting to his disability and struggled to reestablish his sexuality and self-esteem. Despite being in a rehab center, Jay felt he received scant advice about sexual issues:

> *I find it disturbing that in a time of ever-sophisticated advances in rehabilitation medicine, so little attention is paid to an issue as important as an individual's sexuality. As I lay in the hospital waiting for my stumps to heal, I began brooding over what effect my disability was going to have on my relationships with women. But I couldn't find anyone at the hospital who felt comfortable discussing my fears. I became convinced that my leglessness meant I would probably never again know the joys of being intimate with a woman. This thought was as depressing to me as knowing I would never be able to walk again. Fortunately, I found an empathic soul in a physical therapist who was herself an amputee. Her encouragement was invaluable in helping me to resolve my doubts and to see myself in a more positive light.*

Like Gary, Anne, and Jay, there are millions of people with disabilities who eventually discover they can enjoy sexual satisfaction despite their physical limitations. Unfortunately, they often receive very little support or information from parents or rehab professionals who may be too embarrassed or too uncomfortable to attempt a discussion of this issue. Even in an era of sexual enlightenment, a code of silence seems to envelop the issue of disabilities and sexuality.

Judy is another person whose sexuality was "swept under the carpet," because no one expected her to find a mate. A congenital anomaly resulted in Judy being born without legs; she has only short stumps where her legs would have joined her hips.

At age four, Judy was fitted with artificial legs, but, despite frequently practicing with them, the prostheses rubbing against her stumps caused skin pressure that made walking difficult. Even after dozens of adjustments, she found that it was far easier and a lot faster to use a wheelchair. In her parents' home, which wasn't wheelchair accessible, Judy simply scooted around on the floor, using her outstretched arms as substitute feet.

Judy's parents sent her to a private grade school for disabled children, and, when it was time for her to enter junior high, they purposely chose a boarding school for girls. Her parents steadfastly refused to talk to Judy about sex because they felt it was too dangerous, and, as a result, much of her sexual knowledge came from her peers, most of whom knew very little themselves.

Following a late puberty, Judy began to establish her own identity. At about the same time, a school counselor convinced Judy's parents to mainstream her into a regular coed high school in the local public school system. Here she had her first experiences with boys and dating.

Despite Judy's gregarious, outgoing nature, most of her relationships were brief. She often felt that the boys she dated were interested in her only out of curiosity, and, in fact, few asked her out a second time. Even if a boy did express further interest, his parents invariably cautioned him against continuing to date a "crippled" girl. So it was not surprising that when Judy started college she remained a virgin.

During her sophomore year, Judy met Fred, one of the star halfbacks on the football team, and she was immediately smitten. Fred showered her with affection, and they began to see each other regularly. After a number of dates, they discussed having a sexual relationship and eventually rented a motel room so they could spend the night together. But Judy's dream romance quickly turned into a nightmare. Fred was rough and insensitive, intent on his own pleasure at the expense of Judy's. Her first sexual experience was no less than a full-scale disaster.

Shortly after this episode, Fred announced that he thought they should see other people. When Judy pressed him for a reason, Fred admitted that, although he was very fond of her, he had initiated their relationship primarily to satisfy his curiosity and now felt he was becoming too involved. Although he was apologetic, Judy was crushed and for several years afterward avoided intimate relationships.

One hot July day, while on the freeway, Judy's car ran out of gas in the middle of rush-hour traffic. After a few minutes, a police car stopped behind her, and the traffic patrolman, whose name was Murray, walked to the side of her car and offered Judy his assistance.

Judy asked him to call a tow truck for her, which he promptly did. Then, since the temperature was in the high nineties and his patrol car was air-conditioned, Murray invited Judy to sit with him until the truck arrived.

Unfortunately, Judy had left her wheelchair at home, and she wasn't wearing her artificial legs. She explained her predicament to Murray, who, without a moment's hesitation, lifted her in both arms and carried her over to his patrol car. Once inside they laughed about how she had managed to forget *both* the artificial legs and the wheelchair. "It's the only way I could think of to meet handsome policemen," Judy said flirtatiously.

Today, when Judy reflects back on their long marriage, she remembers Murray's unwavering acceptance most of all:

> *Never once in all the time that Murray and I have been together has he ever been critical of my disability. And he hasn't pressured me to change it either. We've grown so used to each other over the years that he never makes any excuses for me, no matter what the situation, not even when he's introducing me to total strangers. It was difficult finding someone who was that accepting, but it was worth the wait.*

As Judy and other people with disabilities have discovered, social and romantic relationships may prove frustratingly elusive for many years, but eventually people and circumstances combine so that both become a reality.

Chapter 3

AN ATTRACTION OF OPPOSITES: DISABLED PEOPLE WITH NONDISABLE D PARTNERS

One in eight people has a physical disability that prevents them from performing basic functions like walking, working, or caring for themselves. But because discomfort and fears about disabilities are so deeply ingrained in our society, a disabled person who wants to become romantically involved with someone who isn't disabled usually has to take the active role in making that relationship a reality. Honest two-way communication about every aspect of the disability seems to be the single most important factor in helping this "attraction of opposites" succeed.

It is especially important that the nondisabled partner fully understand the nature and scope of the disabled partner's physical differences from the beginning. A disability is easier for someone else to accept when all the facts are out in the open. Once a nondisabled person is fully informed about a disability, there is a far greater likelihood that he or she can be support-ive—focusing on the disabled person as a human being first and someone with a disability second.

Assuming that a disability is permanent, one of the first things the nondisabled partner in a romantic relationship must do is accept the fact that the disability is there to stay. Juanita's experiences illustrate why this is so essential.

When she was a teenager in the early 1950s, Juanita be-came partially paralyzed by polio. Eventually her leg muscles atrophied, leaving only bone and fatty tissue.

Many years ago a doctor prescribed leg braces and taught me how to walk with crutches. I practiced every day. But it took such a tremendous effort to get the braces on, and then to stand and walk with all that weight on my legs, that I never became very good at it. So after a while I opted for a wheelchair. I was a lot more comfortable, and I could carry things—something I could really never do on crutches.

I met Phil when I was a receptionist at a small manufacturing company. Phil was our UPS driver, and I saw him at least briefly every day. We became pretty good friends after a while, and then he asked me out for a date. We started seeing a lot of each other, but right from the beginning I don't think he ever accepted the fact that I was disabled. The wheelchair really bothered him. He'd even think of excuses for me to leave it at home when we went out. He'd actually carry me into restaurants and places where we'd go. It felt very uncomfortable to me, but I went along with it anyway because I liked him so much.

Then one day Phil found my old braces and crutches stored in a hall closet and began to insist that I use them. I told him I didn't want to and that I no longer had enough strength to use them. But Phil kept pressuring me, and we got into a big fight about it.

Eventually, we made up, but after that it seemed like every time we'd see each other the topic of my walking again would come up. We began seeing less and less of each other. One day, he was just gone. I cried for a long time. When I finally felt I was over him, I got the braces and the crutches, wheeled them out to the garbage can, and pitched them. It felt exhilarating.

Several years later, Juanita married a man who also had a disability and was much more understanding about her physical limitations.

Perhaps the most difficult challenge in any "mixed" relationship—one that involves disabled and nondisabled partners—is learning how to ignore negative messages from those who would prefer to see the relationship fail. Tuning out these discouraging voices can be even more difficult when they are from family members and relatives.

Greg and Gina had an especially tough time with their families when they were getting together. Everyone offered dire predictions about their future. Greg and Gina met in college after Greg returned from Vietnam, where he had been blinded by a Viet Cong ambush.

Greg was completely unable to adjust. He was embittered about losing his sight and equally bitter about every other aspect of his life. Then he met Gina. She not only brought Greg out of his despair by befriending him but also shared with him her optimistic outlook on life. Over a period of two years, they fell in love and became engaged. However, Gina's family bombarded her with every possible excuse for marrying a man with a disability. "You're marrying him out of pity," her mother said. "Love will never be enough when you're married to someone blind."

Greg's family wasn't much better, actively discouraging him from marrying Gina because they felt she would never be able to understand his problems. "Stick with a disabled woman," Greg's father said. "Otherwise, I give it six months and I'll be paying for a divorce lawyer."

So great were the pressures from both families that Greg and Gina did break up for several months, but eventually they reconciled. This time they skipped the formal engagement period and eloped to Las Vegas.

> *Gina and I have been married for fifteen years. Every chance I get I tease my dad, telling him I think it's probably okay now to spend that money he's been saving for my divorce lawyer.*

Not even well-known people with disabilities have an easy time attracting a nondisabled partner. In July 1987, *Playboy* published an eight-page pictorial featuring the magazine's first disabled Playmate, Ellen Stohl. Ellen has quadriplegia as the result of a single-car accident that irreparably injured her spinal cord. Although she cannot walk and has limited use of her hands, she has almost full strength in her arms. Ellen's quadriplegia is incomplete, meaning that, although she is paralyzed, she experiences almost full sensation in some of the affected parts of her body. She even has some sensation below the level of her injury. She has bladder and bowel sensations, but these muscles are weak, requiring that a rest room always be close by.

After earning a B.A. in communications, Ellen became an advertising copywriter and has since expanded professionally to be an actress, model, spokesperson, and public relations consultant. She now runs her own communications business. Like many people, Ellen admits her most difficult challenge continues to be finding the right partner:

> *Socially I have been treated like anything but a woman—as a child, a disease, an object of pity, or a supergimp. I am seen as a wheelchair first and a person second. If I'm lucky enough to be seen as a person first, it's only superficial; then I'm construed to be so "wonderful" that I'm still not seen as a whole person with vices and virtues, fears and dreams . . . just like everyone else.*

> *Romantically, I don't have much of a problem with men once we*

get past the chair. But to get past that point requires that I be overly outgoing and positive so I can make it okay for the other person. If I'm sad or depressed, people naturally assume it's because of my disability. They see the disability as being the center of my life, when, in fact, it is just the way I am. In relative terms, it's just something different that I have to deal with. None of us is perfect; we must do our best with what we have.

I am very outgoing, so meeting men is somewhat easy for me. Their first reaction, however, is one of disbelief. Either the injury is temporary or I'm faking it. They cannot put together the fact that I have a disability and am sexually attractive at the same time. Once they get past that, they take the attitude that the disability doesn't make a difference. This sounds good but, in fact, it's denial. It does make a difference, but it's just something I have to deal with.

As Ellen points out, at times, no matter how positively a person with a disability interacts with society, he or she will still encounter rejection. Leo, a man with quadriplegia caused by spinal muscular atrophy, cannot use his legs and has very limited motion in his hands and arms. He uses an electric wheelchair and writes on a computer using a mouth stick. He requires assistance from a personal care attendant for many daily activities.

At age 36, Leo has had several friendly relationships but very limited romantic involvements and still no sexual experience—although not from lack of trying. Leo has expressed romantic interest in several women, but, as soon as the relationships started to progress beyond the friendship stage, the women generally found excuses for not continuing. Leo feels his extreme loneliness is a result of his disability, and at times he becomes very discouraged about his lack of prospects:

I have only had friendship-type relationships, never an actual romantic or sexual involvement. It's not that I don't try. There have been many women I've expressed an interest in and tried to get them to be interested in me, but nothing worked out.

Leo's efforts at finding romance have occasionally left him bitter. But he continues to try new and different methods to find a woman with whom he can share a mutual attraction.

I've placed personals ads in newspapers and magazines, and I was always open and honest about my disability. But I never received any responses. Then, as an experiment, I placed an ad in a magazine without mentioning I was disabled. I received three responses. I was so thrilled! But then, when I replied to their letters and explained that I was in a wheelchair, I never heard from any of them again.

Leo has found it best to deal with rejection by honestly appraising the pluses and minuses of his life.

I'm not extremely happy with my life right now, but I am reasonably content. I'm a deeply caring person with no one to care deeply for.

Leo believes that nondisabled people view people with disabilities differently than they do others, often treating them as though they are unable to accept the realities of certain social interactions.

For instance, when a person with a disability becomes romantically interested in a nondisabled partner, the nondisabled person may, if the romantic interest is not mutual, tend to avoid rejecting the disabled person outright for fear of hurting him or her too deeply. It's almost as though the person with a disability is assumed to be incapable of accepting any more "hurt" in life. So the nondisabled person may continue inadvertently to encourage the disabled person, which only results in greater pain later.

Once, I was talking and kidding around with a waitress in a restaurant. One thing led to another, and I asked her if she'd like to go to a movie sometime. She said she'd love to and wrote her phone number on a matchbook for me. The next day when I tried to call her, I got an elderly couple who'd never heard of the girl. I gave her the benefit of the doubt, wrote her a note, and dropped it by the restaurant as I passed. The note had my phone number on it; I asked her to call me. But she never did. That experience hurt me very deeply. I would have rather she said no right from the start.

Most people unfamiliar with disabilities need to be helped past their initial reluctance about becoming involved with a disabled person. That means the burden of proof often rests on the person with the disability, a scenario that can also create some understandable resentment.

Karl is the first to admit that always having to make the first move can "get old," but he also feels doing so is essential for breaking the ice.

Despite my neuromuscular disability, I've always enjoyed a good deal of success with women. I was married twice before I met my present wife, and between marriages I was very active socially and enjoyed several long-term relationships. I found that the secret to my success was making women feel comfortable with my disability, even if they were initially ill at ease with the whole idea.

I think every disabled person, if he or she is seeking romantic relationships, should realize that a disability scares the hell out of most people. So it's up to the disabled person to make the nondisabled person comfortable with that aspect of the relationship.

Dave, 28, suffered a stroke that left him totally paralyzed on one side of his body. As he states,

The most important thing is to think positively about yourself. Don't act like your disability is the world's biggest tragedy. If you do, romantically it will be. Put your best foot forward and act like your disability really doesn't matter. Above all, be friendly and

interested in other people.

Lois, disabled by polio at age 12, agrees, but she also advises against building your entire life around the search for romantic relationships.

I think that the harder someone tries to directly focus on finding social, romantic, or sexual partners, the more difficult it becomes. I would advise any disabled person to balance out their life and become actively involved in work, community projects, recreation, and other activities that involve platonic relationships. Then, make a conscious effort to become interested in the people you come in contact with. Opportunities for social contact will be a natural outgrowth of these activities. Concentrate on becoming a friend first. The romantic part will follow by itself. The same thing holds true whether you're disabled or not.

Still other disabled people have experienced success with less traditional methods for meeting people. Debbie, who is severely disabled by juvenile rheumatoid arthritis, has been married and divorced and is now involved in a new relationship. She offers this advice:

The bar scene is a terrible place to meet people, particularly since it's such a meat market. I would try dating services (ones for both disabled and nondisabled) and personals ads. Keep your options open for everyday opportunities, such as meeting people in the grocery store, in the park, or on the street. I met my ex-husband while I was working in an apartment building as a security guard, and I met my present boyfriend through a personals ad. Meeting people is quite difficult, I feel, especially if you're a disabled female. I have the impression that women are much more open to relationships with disabled men than men are to dating disabled women.

Clearly, the role of open communication cannot be underestimated at the beginning of a relationship in which one of the partners is disabled. It is difficult but important for the disabled person to be totally honest about every aspect of the disability, including physical and sexual limitations and fears of rejection based on previous experiences.

Some of the following questions may help with broaching this admittedly delicate subject:

- Would you like to know more about my disability?
- Does my disability bother you in any way?
- Are other people's reactions to my disability a concern to you?
- Are you wondering about how I feel about my disability?

Through neutral, open-ended questions such as these, a person with a disability can communicate a self-respect that will help put the nondisabled person more at ease.

Karl suggests a method that has worked quite well for him:

Whenever I met a woman I'm attracted to, I simply made the assumption that she was uncomfortable with my disability, at least to some degree. Most women are, having never had relationships with disabled men. It is apparent that I'm disabled, both to her and to me. There is no way I can hide my wheelchair, or obscure the fact that my gait is not quite the same as everyone else's. And, when I talk, that I struggle with a lot of the words. So why should I even try to hide it?

I've found that the best solution is to talk about your disability right off the bat. You can be sure it's on the other person's mind, even if she or he doesn't say so. So the best thing to do is to bring it out into the open and not leave anything unspoken.

I'm not trying to say that your disability should be the only thing you talk about, or that it should be the first topic of conversation. But get it in somewhere, or you'll always be wondering, What is that person really thinking of me?

If a woman's at all interested in me, I find that she'll ask questions. So be ready to answer them. And remember to answer the "hidden" questions she may be very uncomfortable asking you. Things like How did your disability happen? Do you need a lot of help with things? What does it feel like to be disabled?

Karl also advises that a person with a disability should be ready to answer the question he calls The Big One, Can you have sex? In today's society, it's not uncommon for people to carefully consider the issue of sexual compatibility before becoming involved in a potential relationship.

Patricia, a double (arm-leg) amputee as the result of an auto accident, has been in several long-term romantic relationships, including two marriages, and feels attitude is the key to addressing these concerns. Patricia says she always follows her own advice when she enters the nondisabled world in search of a relationship:

> *Always be as independent as you can and positive, never negative, about your disability. A chronic complainer who demands everything be done for him or her is not going to be a good prospect for someone looking for a relationship. Put yourself in the other person's shoes . . . if you saw yourself, would you be attracted?*
>
> *After two divorces and several other relationships, some good, some bad, I've found it best not to leap at a possible relationship just because you might feel this is the only person to show any interest. Don't settle for just anyone. Even though society views people with disabilities as asexual, don't start believing it about yourself. The right person will come along if you work at it.*

While there is sometimes a tendency for people with disabilities to "stay with their own kind" because of the assumption that disabled people are more tolerant of each other's problems—or because they simply don't want to risk more rejection—this approach can be a double-edged sword. There are many more nondisabled people in the world than disabled ones, and the presence or absence of disability in either or both partners really has a minimal bearing on the success of a long-term relationship. If two people genuinely care for each other and have a sincere and mutual commitment, it makes little difference whether one or both (or neither, for that matter) has a disability.

As the individuals in this chapter illustrate, the need for sexual expression is never lost as the result of an injury or illness. Every person, regardless of gender, age, or disability, is a sexual being. Furthermore, every person has the right to sexual expression, and there is hardly anyone who is too disabled to have some pleasure from his or her sexuality—with a partner if possible, alone if necessary. It is up to each person to discover the kind of sexual expression that works for him or her and the best way to achieve it.

Sidebar to go here

Breaking the Ice with a Person Who Has a Disability

Diane Piastro offers these excellent recommendations for relating to people with disabilities:

- If you offer assistance, be guided by the individual's response *before* going ahead.
- Talk directly to the disabled person. Don't ask a companion to speak for him or her.

FOR A PERSON WITH A HEARING IMPAIRMENT:
You may need to get the person's attention by tapping his shoulder or waving. Shouting won't help; written notes will.
If the person reads lips, look directly at him or her and speak expressively. If one word isn't understood, try another.

FOR A PERSON WITH A SPEECH IMPAIRMENT
Give this individual your unhurried attention.
Do not complete the person's sentences. Repeat what you understand.
Don't pretend to understand. And don't be afraid to ask the person to repeat what he or she has just said.

FOR A PERSON WITH A VISION IMPAIRMENT
Don't speak loudly, this person hears as well as you do.
Identify yourself; let the person know when you are going to leave.
If you assist someone, walk slightly ahead and let the person take your arm. This allows you to guide rather than propel.

FOR A PERSON WITH A MOBILITY IMPAIRMENT
Don't lean on a person's wheelchair. It is an extension of the person who uses it.
When talking for more than a few minutes, place yourself at the wheelchair user's eye level.
When you plan to go out, make a phone call ahead to be sure of handicapped parking, a step-free entrance, et cetera.

Chapter 4

BUILDING SELF-ESTEEM IN
AN UNACCEPTING WORLD

Self-esteem, the feelings we all have about our physical and emotional selves, is a vital component in how we face the challenges of life. When basic self-respect is eroded, good relationships with others are hard to develop and maintain, inner peace remains elusive, and anger, depression, and addictive behaviors become commonplace.

It is not difficult to understand why someone's self-esteem may suffer when he or she becomes disabled or has been disabled since childhood. The physically disabled are routinely denied acceptance in every area, from transportation and schooling to employment and social interactions. In many media depictions, the disabled person is either a pathetic victim who deserves only pity or charity or a brave fighter who triumphs over his or her disabling condition. In a world that cherishes youth, beauty, vitality, good health, and self-reliance, people with disabilities have to battle constantly for the fundamental human right simply to be who they really are.

These unfortunate attitudes persist because nondisabled people typically expect that everyone they confront on a daily basis will appear to be "normal." They will walk normally, speak clearly, not have a vision or hearing impairment, have the usual level of physical stamina, and be able to follow the train of a normal conversation with ease. Any variation leads others to define individuals in highly negative terms. These deeply ingrained prejudices date back to the days of ancient Athens and Sparta, when any baby who had a disability was left on the side of a mountain to die. Even now, in some parts of the United States, physical impairments are viewed as an indication of the disabled person's sin—or the parents' sin—and considered a form of punishment, atonement, or both.

Nowhere is rejection by the nondisabled society more evident than in attitudes about the sexuality of the disabled, and, naturally, these negative feelings have a profound effect on quality of life. Even when the person with a disability has not been socially isolated or has been able to develop good social skills, societal norms and expectations about sexuality and disability are often so damaging that the person is left feeling unattractive, undesirable, and completely neutered.

As noted in the book *The Sexually Oppressed*, edited by Harvey and Jean Gochros,

He or she may actually deprive himself [or herself] of sexualized thoughts or actions believing these are inappropriate for a disabled person. In its place are feelings of ugliness, self-contempt and fear that are as great an internal barrier to satisfying sexuality (no matter what the mode) as are the real external barriers to the achievement of these satisfactions, such as social isolation, lack of recreational opportunities and architectural and attitudinal barriers.

In one all-too-familiar scenario related by the Gochroses, a 55-year-old single accountant who had been disabled in childhood by polio sought help for his feelings of self-loathing and despair, which he saw as directly related to his inability to express himself sexually. Although physically and financially independent, he lived with his parents, who intruded on all aspects of his life to the extent that he had little privacy even to masturbate. This man repeatedly expressed the conviction that he had nothing to offer in relationships and that no woman would want him because of his disability.

How can a person with a disability effectively fight society's negative messages, build self-esteem, and reject conscious and unconscious feelings of unworthiness? Clearly, it is a difficult and challenging task. But it is also a rewarding experience that can form the basis for more positive interactions in every aspect of social and romantic relationships. The advice offered by Edmund Hopper and William Allen in *Sex Education for Physically Handicapped Youth*, a self-help book for disabled teenagers, makes a good starting point for people of any age.

> [As a person with a disability,] you can choose to have a proud, positive self-concept or a weak, distorted opinion of yourself. To have a strong self-image is not to deny that you have a disabling condition. It's just to understand that the disabled parts of your body are only part of your whole body machine that makes you the very special human being that you are.

Maintaining this inner dialogue with yourself, a conversation filled with calm reassurance and positive self-affirmation, is only part of the battle. This foundation must be strengthened by constant reminders from within that a disabled person has every right to a complete and fulfilling life, including a sexual life, no matter how he or she outwardly varies from society's ideals of physical attractiveness. A person with a disability has to both act and feel confident, letting others know that he or she will not be treated as a second-class citizen.

Some methods for creating this positive impression include

- Sharing information with others about your strengths and the things you like about yourself, through either discussion or direct experience
- Not overcompensating for insecurities and self-doubts by trying to monopolize conversation
- Risking social rejection at least once a week by initiating meaningful contact with one new person
- Practicing active listening and really paying attention to what the other person is saying; drawing him or her out by asking open-ended questions
- Keeping the conversation upbeat rather than negative, affirming rather than complaining
- Maintaining good grooming habits and wearing a hairstyle and clothing that are flattering. If you're unsure about your appearance, ask for honest feedback from someone whose opinion you trust
- Taking a sincere interest in others, and letting them know what you like and admire about them
- Keeping emotional neediness in check so you don't alienate people by clinging or manipulating
- Learning how to behave in a loving manner toward another person without smothering him or her out of jealousy or fear of rejection
- Staying interesting and well-informed about a variety of subjects. This means keeping up with what's going on in the world around you, especially in popular culture and entertainment, two subjects that have seemingly endless universal appeal

- Becoming more active in ways that are stimulating or energizing, through a group activity that interests you, a hobby you can share, exercise, adult education classes, or community outreach programs
- Obtaining current information about sex, and getting more in touch with your sexuality by masturbation, reading erotica, fantasizing, or doing whatever feels comfortable to you
- Developing good sexual communication skills so you and your prospective (or current) partner can enhance your relationship through mutually satisfying experiences
- Seeking out sexual counseling or psychotherapy from a qualified professional, who, if at all possible, has been recommended to you by another person with a disability

In the words of one woman who was initially reluctant to go into psychotherapy because she felt "only crazy people have to do that,"

Professional counseling helped me immensely. It helped me in finding out who I am, what life is about, and in accepting myself as a sexual person who just happens to have a disability. I used to use my disability as an "excuse" for not being sexual, not expressing my own sexuality. Now I've learned that disabled people have a right to express themselves sexually, the same as anyone else. To not do this is cheating yourself out of one of life's greatest pleasures.

Although more than 60 percent of rehabilitation counselors are still untrained in sex counseling and only one counselor in five reports initiating discussion about sexuality with disabled clients, this trend is slowly changing. There is a growing awareness among counseling and rehabilitation professionals that directly addressing the sexual needs of disabled people is essential to helping build a positive self-concept. We can only hope that this welcome trend continues and that many more people with disabilities will be able to take advantage of knowl-edgeable, sensitive counseling about this important concern.

Chapter 5

THE JOY OF DISABLED SEX—FOR COUPLES

*A*s people with disabilities have often shared with us, being sexually expressive may sometimes prove difficult, but doing so is satisfying, worthwhile, and extremely helpful in making an overall psychological adjustment to any disability.

As noted in the book *The Sexually Oppressed*, edited by Harvey and Jean Gochros, a person with a disability may experience loss of sensation in the genitals or other areas; be unable to move legs, arms, pelvis; suffer from bowel or bladder incontinence; or have involuntary spastic movements. A woman may have chronic pain and an inability to move certain joints, such as the hips. A man may be unable to have an erection, or the erection may last only a short time and he may be unable to ejaculate. What each of these physiological realities means is that the disabled person and his or her sexual partner may have to consider changing the timing of their sexual intimacy, the positions they use, the type of sexual activities they engage in, their means of contraception, and the nature of their communication surrounding sexual activities.

Tom and Randi's relationship is living proof of a saying that holds true for many people with disabilities and their partners—"Where there's a will there's a way."

While still in high school, Tom, who was an avid rock climber, slipped and fell thirty feet down a mountain during a weekend camping trip. Although he suffered a severe head injury that left him in a coma for several weeks, Tom's doctors held out the hope that chances for a complete recovery were excellent. However, just before emerging completely from his comatose state, Tom suffered a setback. The shock of the injury had caused *status epilepticus,* a condition in which the electrical impulses inside the brain are short-circuited. As a result, Tom suffered a series of severe grand mal epileptic seizures that lasted for several days.

The seizures took a heavy toll, and Tom was left partially paralyzed in his arms and legs. Most of his muscles were spastic, leaving him unable to coordinate conscious movement. Every joint in his body was stiff and painful, and he couldn't stand, walk, or take care of his daily needs.

Whereas before the accident Tom had shown tremendous promise as an artist and musician and had enjoyed photography, poetry writing, and horseback riding, his brain damage completely robbed him of his ability to speak, read, or write. Today, Tom communicates with a yes-no finger system, a smattering of sign language, and a limited repertoire of facial expressions. However, he fully understands what is said, and he is completely aware of his surroundings.

Tom and Randi met when he was transferred to a large rehabilitation hospital a few years later for additional therapy. Randi, a registered nurse, helped manage his treatment.

Tom's and my nurse-patient relationship grew into a nice friend-ship during the months he was at the hospital. After he left, I began writing to him (his Mom read him the letters), and then I began visiting. It felt a little weird at first, because I was afraid of others questioning my motives. But I really liked his family, and our relationship grew and deepened. Although I only see Tom once a month on a weekend because we live so far apart, I plan to move closer to him soon. We make a good couple, complimenting each other in lots of ways. Although Tom is severely disabled, I can feel the strength of his intelligence and personality very keenly, and we enjoy each other a lot.

For about the last year, Tom and I have been intimate sexually. It is in this one area that I've seen Tom change from a shy boy into a confident man. These changes have carried over into other parts of our relationship and into his ability to cope with his disability and the world in general.

Tom has said that, after his accident, the one thing he missed more than anything else was intimacy . . . in personal relationships, with his family, and in sex. Because of his disability, he was no longer able to see himself as a whole man. I'm happy to say that, since we've become lovers, much of that feeling has changed.

When Tom and I make love, it is a unique sexual experience, unlike any other I've ever imagined or heard about. I must be the active partner, although Tom frequently initiates. It bothers him that he is unable to grab me, take me in certain positions, French kiss, perform oral sex on me, or use his hands to stimulate me. But I am very happy with what we are able to do, and I focus on that.

We do what any other couple does sexually, within the limits of our physical abilities and emotional comfort zone. We play. We explore. We talk about sexual things here and there throughout the day. I buy him sexy magazines, and we look at them together. I wear sexy clothes and lingerie for him. And sometimes when he doesn't want to and I do, I take a bit of advantage of his disability and just stick

43

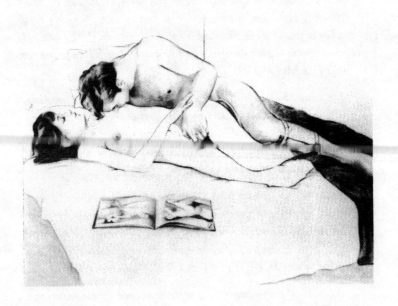

his hand where I want it. Tom seems to love that and gets a big kick out of it.

Intercourse isn't simple, but we try to be creative about it. Usually we start out with me on top straddling him. Then I grab Tom in a bear hug and roll him over on top of me. We come to rest with pillows under my bottom. I get a good grip on his bottom and help him in his thrusting motions. Tom frequently has muscle spasms during sex, but we just ride them out. I put his fingers inside of me, and then we slow everything down. Like the song says, Tom is a "lover with a slow hand." It takes us a long time to make love, often several hours. But it's a slow, easy form of lovemaking. And when the peak finally comes, we seem to be together in each other's souls.

I've had my doubts, sure. Most of them come when I ask myself, "Am I crazy for loving someone who's so disabled? Am I so insecure I can't find anyone else?" My friends' reactions and other people's judgments haven't helped much. So I've had to do much self-evaluation, knowing that, if we marry, we'll probably never be rich, and he'll never be able to screw my brains out. But I've dated lots of men, different kinds of men, so I know what's out there. And Tom's the only one who's made me feel nice, peaceful, and special. He laughs at my jokes and appreciates everything I do for him. So I have a lot of motivation in accepting the difficulties.

Randi's satisfying relationship with Tom shows that even people with severe disabling conditions can experience the joy of being romantic and sexual. Tom may not be able to contribute as much as he'd like to physically, but, because of Randi's willingness to be flexible, their relationship has survived and flourished.

Because of the wide range of disabilities, it is often difficult to predict how each person's specific condition will affect sexuality. Most people with disabilities experience at least some differences in the way they are sexual. Yet others, depending on their situations, may experience no differences at all. Those who cannot engage in the usual sexual positions, for instance, are often able to make the necessary adaptations.

Although Doug has quadriplegia as the result of an accident and is completely paralyzed from the armpits down, he can still have erections. Although he is unable to experience sexual feeling in his penis, touching it can produce a reflex erection, which is caused by automatic physical responses rather than by sexual stimuli. However, the result is the same—a sufficiently stiff erection that allows Doug to have intercourse. Although he cannot feel his penis during intercourse, the sexual stimulation Doug experiences is able to produce an orgasm. Doug says that he "feels" sexual release in other ways and that these sensations are equally satisfying to him.

Although before his accident Doug's sexuality was focused on intercourse, now he finds that foreplay, cuddling, and kissing are immensely satisfying. And when he watches his lover as they passionately make love and she climaxes, Doug climaxes too. "I've found that giving is its own reward," Doug says, somewhat mischievously.

I don't allow my disability to prevent me from having a great sex life. However, my ability to sustain intercourse for long periods of time or to be in the male-superior position is somewhat limited. Sometimes I miss these things, but not very often. When I do have orgasms, I am unable to feel the physical sensation or the usual throbbing feeling in my genitals. But I do receive a similar "rush" from oral sex—going down on a woman is very pleasurable for me, as is massage, kissing, making out, and long sessions of togetherness and snuggling.

Most women like oral sex very much; I've had few complaints and have learned to be something of an "expert" at it. For sustained intercourse, my lover has to be on top, straddling me from a kneeling position with me flat on my back. She must be very careful to very slowly ease herself onto my penis, guiding it into her vagina; otherwise we run the risk of me losing the erection. Once I'm inside her, it really makes no difference, since I usually stay hard until I have my orgasm.

I find that for me manual and oral stimulation, combined with intercourse, provides the most pleasurable sex. I also love cunnilingus and extended foreplay, and I've experimented with different positions. But, for me, sex is usually best when my partner and I take a lot of time with each other, express loving feelings, and are very careful not to rush things.

Ben is another person with a disability who has made the adjustments necessary to enjoy a good sex life. Disabled since birth by congenital spinal muscular atrophy, Ben has quadriplegia characterized by nearly total motor paralysis. He cannot feel his legs, and his arms are extremely weak, but he has full sensory feeling elsewhere.

Ben is able to feed himself, provided that his meal is positioned directly in front of him. However, he relies on a personal care attendant for dressing, personal hygiene, meal preparation, and transportation. Ben uses an electric wheelchair at all times, although even the minimal exertion of pushing on the control stick can drain his energy.

Despite his physical limitations, Ben considers himself a fortunate man. Making friends had always come easily to him, although for much of his life romantic involvements proved elusive. Most of the women in whom he was interested preferred to stay "just friends."

Then, while in his senior year at college, Ben met Jeanne, a graduate student. Ben's pleasant personality, coupled with Jeanne's easygoing acceptance of other people's differences, helped spark a romantic relationship. Ben and Jeanne became intimate not long after they started dating. It was Ben's first sexual experience, and he wondered if he would be able to please a woman. Because of masturbatory activity in his high school years, he had little doubt of his own ability to respond sexually.

Ben and Jeanne began their sexual relationship slowly and carefully. What sexual activities Ben could not manage physically, Jeanne made up for by blending her abilities with his limitations. Ben's weak muscles and the fact that he exhausts easily, for example, make it nearly impossible for him to be on top during intercourse. So together the couple has developed their own sexual style, with Jeanne exerting most of the physical effort. Both seem pleased with the results of their creativity.

Even though I'm paralyzed, I'm fortunate that I still have full sensation and that I'm able to do anything sexually that any other man can do. But, because of the weakness in my muscles, we cannot use certain positions for sex. I even have problems giving hugs, since I first have to ask, "Sweetheart, will you help me put my arms around you?" Even then, I can't hug and hold Jeanne as forcefully as I'd like. Our sex has to stay soft and gentle too. Which is fine with Jeanne, because that's what she likes.

Most of the sexual positions we use involve the woman on top taking the active role. We make love with me lying flat on my back, with me sitting up in a sideless chair, and even with me in my wheelchair once the sides are removed. In each of these positions, Jeanne is either facing me or with her backside toward me. We've also found that the side positions work well, either face to face or with me entering from behind. We also use one other position quite a bit where I sit on the couch and Jeanne lies prone across my lap.

I think it's extremely important to be flexible in your view of what constitutes "sex" when some of the basic positions are difficult or impossible. The ability to be loving and sexually expressive is much more important than just having intercourse for the hell of it. And a lot more fun, too.

In her *Sourcebook for the Disabled*, Glorya Hale describes the many ways in which a disabled person can remain sexually active:

Many disabled men and women can achieve a physical orgasm. Others, depending on the disabling condition or the extent and location of their injury, do not have the physical sensation of orgasm, but, because the brain can work independently of the genitals in generating an erotic experience, they do have feelings of sexual fulfillment.

Those who became disabled as adults may remember the sensations they had and can mentally recreate them. Even people who never experienced an orgasm are often able to fantasize one which is both intense and enjoyable. By making love with the lights on, using mirrors to enable them to see their partner's reactions, talking about what they are doing and feeling and then amplifying and integrating all the sensations in their minds, many people are able to achieve a high level of fulfillment.

Other people, including many nondisabled people, find close personal warmth and body contact without orgasm deeply and fully satisfying. Although the aim of most sexual expression may be reaching orgasm, it's clearly not necessary to have an orgasm for both partners to achieve intense sexual satisfaction.

Chapter 6

SEXUAL VARIATIONS AND ALTERNATIVES

*T*here are literally hundreds of ways to express sexual*
feeling, and none of them is right or wrong. Any kind of sexual
expression that is enjoyable and fulfilling is right, if it is acceptable to both partners.

It's wise to ignore the "marriage manual" formula, which
views some sexual activities as foreplay, some as afterplay, and
only penile-vaginal penetration as "the real thing." Instead,

---

*Much of the material in this chapter as well as the technical definitions of specific
disabilities throughout this book were derived from Glorya Hale's landmark work *The
Sourcebook for the Disabled*, published by addington Press in 1979. Although the book is now
out of print, and the publisher has long ago ceased to publish, *The Sourcebook for the Disabled*
should be read by anyone who is disabled or who interacts with someone who is. Fortunately, it can still be found on the shelves of many local and academic libraries.

sexual expression should be regarded as an individual experience without rules or scorecards and with the only goal being to provide pleasure for both partners. Anything is acceptable, for however long and in whatever sequence you and your partner prefer. Let things happen at whatever pace is good for both of you. The object is to enjoy yourselves and to get the greatest pleasure by making the most of what you have, not bemoaning the functions you may lack.

Sexual sensation is possible in areas other than those which are generally regarded as "erogenous zones." There is no area of the body which is not, or cannot become, responsive to erotic stimulation.

It's important to know what your options are and to experiment with various kinds of sexual expression to discover what is most exciting and satisfying. But, again, the key to a good sexual relationship for any couple, nondisabled or disabled, is communication. You and your partner must convey to each other what feels good and what is and is not pleasurable.

Arousal can begin well before actual sexual activity. Talking and touching while eating or drinking, kissing and caressing each other while watching television or listening to music can be sexually arousing for many people. Others find that they enjoy having their sexual imaginations awakened as a prelude to lovemaking by looking together at erotic pictures or reading erotica (some people might call it pornography, but don't let that influence you) or talking about their fantasies and what they are going to do when they get into bed. Other possibilities include taking a bath or shower together, slipping into bed together nude, or sipping on some wine or brandy. It can also help establish a more romantic mood in the bedroom (if that is where two people choose to make love) to put freshly laundered sheets on the bed, scent the air with incense or perfume, and remove from the night table the rows of prescription medicines that are so often part of the life of a person with a disability.

Of course, when one or both partners is disabled, it may not be quite so easy, or fast, to get into bed and be ready for sexual activity, but many couples find that they can maintain sexual arousal by incorporating some of their preparations into their lovemaking.

Once you're in a position for sexual activity, what to do and how to do it are up to you and your partner. There are no rules. Environmental stimulation can heighten enjoyment and should not be overlooked. Some people enjoy total darkness, for example, while others like to make love by candlelight or soft light and use mirrors so that they can watch each other's reactions.

Simple body contact, the sensation of skin on skin, can give both partners great comfort and pleasure. Time spent holding and stroking each other can greatly enhance the feeling of intimacy and increase gratification. Giving a massage can be exciting for both. This can be done with your hands or with a vibrator. It's not necessary to have much manual dexterity if you know where to touch your partner to give him or her pleasure.

Some women can have an orgasm, or can be brought very close to one, by having their breasts stimulated by a partner's hand or mouth. Some men, too, have great sensitivity in their nipples and get intense pleasure when they are licked, nibbled, or rubbed.

You can use any part of your body, including your mouth, to rub and stroke your partner's body and to stimulate him or her to orgasm. A finger, thumb, wrist, elbow, or knee can be used to stimulate the clitoris. The penis can be enveloped by a hand, an armpit, the breasts pressed together, or the buttocks.

Although sexual intercourse is neither the only nor necessarily the most gratifying sexual activity, it is the most common. Penile-vaginal penetration can be accomplished in many positions, limited only by individual abilities and inclinations. Obviously, your disability will influence the positions you are able to use. Different positions also have different advantages. Some are better for achieving movement, while others are more passive. Some can decrease any inconvenience caused by a urine collection device. You have to experiment to discover which positions are best for you.

A creative approach and time allowed for trial and error will enable you to find comfortable positions. For some couples, the best way to begin is to find a position which is comfortable and then adapt it to intercourse. Keep various-sized cushions handy. They can make some positions more comfortable or even possible.

Vaginal lubrication, which usually happens naturally during sexual arousal, can be affected by the time needed to become aroused, a vaginal infection, the Pill, or a disabling condition. Sometimes, extra lubrication will help make penetration easier, and it should always be used when a catheter is left in place. The lubrication should be water soluble; petroleum jelly, which does not dissolve completely and can promote infections, should never be used.

Even if genital feeling is lacking, the anus may remain sensitive and therefore become more important in sexual arousal. Men and women often find anal stimulation exciting, and some women enjoy the sensation of anal touching and probing during vaginal intercourse.

The mouth is as much a sexual organ as the genitals and can excite and give great pleasure. Some people find that their lips and tongues are more sensitive to touch and temperature than any other parts of their bodies. Certainly, the sensations received from the smell, taste, and texture of your partner's skin can heighten your pleasure. The tongue or the mouth on a sensitive area such as the ear, neck, wrist, or breast can be extremely exciting.

Some people feel timid about oral-genital stimulation. Fellatio, when the mouth and tongue are used to stimulate a man's penis and the surrounding area, and cunnilingus, when the woman's vulva and clitoris are stimulated with the mouth and tongue, are positive, mutually pleasurable sexual options.

For people with disabilities who cannot physically manage intercourse, or for whom intercourse proves too strenuous, oral sex offers an excellent compromise. When performed with tenderness and without inhibition, oral sex can provide as much satisfaction as penile-vaginal penetration.

Rob is disabled by a spinal cord injury that left him with quadriplegia after a drinking bout ended when his jeep plunged down a steep embankment. Sex had always played an important role in Rob's life, and it continued to do so after his injury.

Rob can have intermittent erections, but they are usually short-lived, and he cannot depend on them for sustained sexual activity. But Rob is an enthusiastic advocate of oral sex and considers himself a highly proficient lover in this regard. His story illustrates not only how someone can continue to be unabashedly sexual despite a disability but how skillful oral sex can be as fulfilling to a partner as traditional intercourse.

Rob felt especially sexually compatible with Sonya, his second wife:

> Sonya and I were into everything sexual. We tried everything there was to try. Light bondage, toys, vibrators, anal sex. For a time we were even into group sex and swinging with another couple. We had two crips (the guys) and two walkies (the women). It was great.

> But our best sex came from me satisfying Sonya orally. I quickly learned to be an expert at what I call tongue-in-groove sex. Those were the most satisfying sexual experiences of my life. Even when I do have an erection, I can't really feel anything. It looks great plunging in and out of my wife, and it pleases her, but I get little out of it other than knowing that she likes it. But with oral sex, it's a completely different story.

> I get my biggest and most intense sexual thrills by watching my

wife respond to my oral lovemaking. The visual aspects are more intense than any sexual pleasures I had before my injury. I don't actually come like this, but the excitement of me burying my mouth and tongue in her body and being able to watch the way she gets worked up into a sexual frenzy is plenty for me. When she has one of her mind-wrenching, screaming orgasms, I come right along with her.

Rob feels that the secret to satisfying oral sex is to allow each partner enough time to experience prolonged periods of pleasure and satisfaction.

We probably make love a lot slower than other people. We may have sex for two hours or more, and at least half that time is spent with my head between her legs. When we're ready to start oral contact, she places several firm pillows under her hips to get her vagina up really high where I can get to her. Sometimes, she sits on the edge of a table or desk with a pillow under her, and I stay in my wheelchair with her vagina exposed at about the level of my head. She spreads her legs wide, sometimes holding her knees back to her chest or maybe with her legs draped over my shoulders and her feet resting on the wheelchair. This position gives me the best access to everywhere that gives her pleasure.

I start kissing her vaginal lips, inner thighs, and pubic mound slowly and carefully. Then, as she begins to respond, I gently begin to lick, slowly at first, but with ever-increasing intensity. My tongue gently moves up and down, side to side. Carefully, because this produces very intense reactions, I lick over and around the clitoris in slow, circular motions.

I also try to use a wide variety of oral techniques. Instead of just licking and kissing, I take Sonya's vaginal lips into my mouth, sucking on them tenderly. Then I move to the clitoris, placing my whole mouth over this sensitive area, and I suck gently on the now erect nub. By now her entire vaginal area is covered with a combination of her secretions and my saliva, and everything is very wet and slippery. Then I use my tongue not only to lick but to probe into her. I enter her vagina with my tongue and go in as deep as I can, in and out, more licking, more sucking, then plunge in once again with my tongue.

Then I start using one finger of one hand to enter her as deeply as I can, then another finger. With the other hand I reach up and fondle her breasts, gently pinching and pulling on her aroused nipples. All the while I'm sliding my fingers in and out, in and out. But my mouth is still active, having never left her clitoris. I'm sucking and licking at the same time I'm plunging in and out of her with one hand, playing with her nipples with the other.

The visual aspects are incredible. Sonya is writhing with sexual arousal and moaning with pure pleasure. And I'm just as excited as she is. I can see the flutter of her belly as she feels every flick of my tongue, every movement of my fingers inside her. As she starts to come, her breasts flush and move up and down, and the veins on her neck pulse. Then when she does come, she pushes herself harder into my face and onto my fingers. And I go over the brink at exactly the same time.

Ed is another man with quadriplegia who relies on oral sex as a favorite lovemaking technique:

Before my disability, my preference was sexual intercourse. I'd engage in oral sex primarily to please my lover. Now it's my favorite kind of sex, and the best part is that I'm capable of being a fully active sex partner this way. My girlfriend is ecstatic over the way I go down on her. Kiddingly, she once told me that I have "the nicest face she ever came across."

I've licked my girlfriend all over, genitals and anus, but mainly concentrating on the clitoris, for up to an hour at a time. We do this in any position that's mutually comfortable—including her on the kitchen table or on the edge of a high bed while I'm in my wheelchair. Our favorite way to finish up is with her having an orgasm after a few minutes of me gently sliding my thumb in and out of her wet vagina while delicately licking her clitoris. This produces an earth-shaking orgasm for her and, since I have about 80 percent feeling in my thumb, I can feel the excitement and throbbing inside her as it happens. For me, this produces its own sexual release, not unlike orgasm. It feels different, but it's just as satisfying.

My best advice to other disabled people and their lovers is to concentrate on mutual pleasure, trust, and patience. Accept your physical limitations without complaint, and adapt your sexual techniques to meet your partner's needs. Be positive about sex, and, above all, hang on to your sense of humor.

Making love is, for every couple, whether nondisabled or disabled, a very private part of their relationship and one that develops and changes to suit their personal choices and needs. Bookstores and libraries are full of books that detail and illustrate an infinite variety of ways to achieve sexual gratification; no practice which is acceptable to both partners should be overlooked. A loving, determined, and resourceful couple, regardless of the disability of one or both partners, can find ways to fulfill their sexual needs and to give both partners maximum pleasure.

Sexual Techniques and Possibilities

In the same way that various aids can make activities such as driving, typing, eating, bathing, and cooking easier or possible for people with disabilities, there are aids and devices which can be used to increase sexual pleasure. Most of these are readily available from sex stores and mail-order companies (see Appendix 3) and were designed for and are extensively used by nondisabled men and women. So there's no stigma attached to buying them or using them.

A vibrator can add new dimension to sexual enjoyment,

and there are many types available. Those that fit on the hand can be used for facial or body massage. Battery-powered penile-shaped vibrators are especially good for vaginal or clitoral stimulation since they are quite lightweight and, if necessary, can be modified to accommodate a limited grasp. And a new type of vibrator, which is built into a stationary "saddle" base and therefore isn't dependent on hand dexterity, has recently been advertised in mainstream sexuality magazines such as *Libido* (P.O. Box 146721, Chicago, IL 60614). The only drawback is expense; the standard model of this vibrator costs several hundred dollars.

When a man is not able to have an erection, he can give his partner the sensation of penetration and penile-vaginal stimulation by using a penis stiffener or a dildo. A penis stiffener, which is usually made of a formed piece of hard rubber, fits over the penis and makes penetration possible. A dildo is an artificial penis made of plastic or rubber which can be strapped on above the penis or held in the hand.

Some couples find that a water bed, by increasing body motion, adds to the pleasures of lovemaking. Water beds have also proved excellent for the prevention of pressure sores. A water bed can rest on a sturdy bed frame, but it's extremely heavy, so be sure the floor is strong enough to support the weight. A heating unit should accompany any water bed you buy.

Massage oils are available in a variety of flavors and fragrances; they can serve as lubricants, and they enhance sensations of smell and taste. Like other aids, they can heighten sexual excitement.

Preparation for Lovemaking

Spontaneous sex is not possible for everyone, nor does everyone consider it desirable. For some people, a fair amount of preparation is necessary before lovemaking can begin. When joints are stiff, for example, it's often helpful to have a warm shower before making love. And, while cleanliness is important for everyone's sexual enjoyment, it's particularly so for those who wear catheters or devices to collect urine. (Neither urine collection devices nor catheters, incidentally, need stand in the way of physical intimacy. Depending on your attitude, such a device can be a nuisance or no trouble at all.)

If you're not able to do much yourself to get ready for bed, your partner may want to help you. It's your responsibility to let him or her know what has to be done and how to do it. Much in lovemaking, however, depends on mental processes, and it might be difficult for a partner to feel romantic with someone whose catheter he or she has just changed. The important thing is that you and your partner know each other's feelings about such matters. Then you can decide together how or whether he or she should help with your personal care.

If you both decide it's best that your partner doesn't assist you, or if he or she can't manage alone, an attendant or another third person can help you wash and undress, attach any appliances, and get into bed (see Chapter 9). This does, of course, intrude on privacy, and it's not exactly convenient to have a third person involved in your sex life. Also, the comfort of your attendant must also be considered. But with planning and good, honest communication between you, your partner, and your attendant, you should be able to work out a happy solution. Many other people have.

Chapter 7

THE JOY OF DISABLED
SEX—ALONE

Masturbating

fter being shrouded in puritanical guilt and mystery for centuries, masturbation is now recognized as a healthy and normal act for women and men at any age. In fact, masturbation is currently enjoying a kind of renaissance as a powerful form of sexual self-affirmation—at least partially as a result of greater emphasis on safe sexual practices throughout the world since the AIDS crisis began.

Masturbation is a celebration of the sexual spirit within us all and as such deserves as much attention and respect as intercourse or other expressions of sexuality. Whether enjoyed alone or with a partner, masturbation allows the fulfillment of essential human needs in a positive and pleasurable way. Especially for people with disabilities, masturbation may be the first step toward acknowledging and coming to terms with their sexuality after years of asexual "programming" by everyone from parents and teachers to institutional administrators and rehabilitation professionals.

As Glorya Hale writes in *The Sourcebook for the Disabled*,

> Masturbation is a way to explore your own body, to get to know it and understand it. And masturbation can involve parts of the body other than the genitals. Touching and stroking yourself can help you to learn what your body can feel and do. When you know what feels good and gives you pleasure, it may help you to communicate your preferences to a partner.

Unfortunately, it is also a fact of life that, because disabled people are often rejected as romantic partners, masturbation may be the only alternative to abstinence for long periods. For Debby, disabled by juvenile rheumatoid arthritis for more than 28 years, masturbation offers welcome relief from celibacy:

> *Whenever I don't have a partner, I masturbate frequently. It's amazing how good masturbation coupled with sexual memories or fantasies can make me feel. But masturbation isn't always possible for someone like me with limited movement. To solve this problem, I taped a vibrator to a long handle so that I could move it around more easily. I find it really works well.*

Regardless of the disability, there are as many ways to masturbate as there are to express yourself sexually. Adult mail-order catalogs are an excellent source for vibrators and sex toys purchased discreetly, and several specialized independent living catalogs (see Appendix 3) sell adaptive mitts and handles so that these items can be used comfortably. Other variations on masturbation include reading erotic books or watching adult

movies, fantasizing, watching your own movements in a mirror, or relying on the sensual feel of certain fabrics, textures, or leathers.

Contrary to popular belief, orgasm is not the true goal of masturbation; rather, the goal is to express sexual feelings and enjoy a self-affirming, sexually fulfilling act. To truly enjoy masturbation, it is especially important to free yourself from the idea that self-stimulation is in any way unhealthy, immoral, or emotionally immature. In fact, masturbation is a source of pleasure, to be learned and enjoyed for its own sake. It releases sexual tension, keeps sexual desire alive, and can preserve the integrity of sexual functioning.

Visiting Prostitutes

Because they lack an available partner, some people with disabilities seek out prostitutes. Although we cannot specifically endorse sex with a prostitute, primarily because it results in being vulnerable to criminal activity, sexually transmitted diseases, or legal problems, it is a viable means for sexual satisfaction. The coldness of sex with a prostitute may bear little resemblance to the closeness of lovemaking with someone you care for and cherish. But, historically, it has remained a more or less accepted way for some people to be sexual in our society.

Mel, a 26-year-old man with paraplegia caused by spina bifida, started frequenting prostitutes because of difficulties finding a woman who would have a physical relationship with him.

> *Despite my paralysis, I wanted and needed sex, and prostitutes seemed like the easy way out. I was a virgin, yet I had this driving need to find out what sex was all about. I started to go to this very kind and sincere call girl who taught me a lot about sex and about my physical capabilities as a man. Now that I have my own steady girlfriend, I no longer see this woman, but she calls me every now*

and then just to see how I'm doing. It's rare to find a hooker that truly cares, but this one did. I'm toying with idea of inviting her to my wedding, assuming that my girlfriend allows it!

Rob is a man with quadriplegia who began frequenting houses of prostitution when he was in high school. Most of his sexual education was gained through prostitutes.

I started going to prostitutes when I was 16. Although I was in a wheelchair, I was always really popular with the girls at school, but I never got to the point where any of them would have sex with me. We'd talk about it a lot, but when it came to the reality of taking off our clothes and getting in bed, they all chickened out. I came to the sad realization that the only way to get dependable sex, regular sex, was to purchase it.

There were several local cathouses in my state, where it's legal, mostly catering to the high-dollar tourist and convention trade. The hard-core hookers worked the houses in the winter. Then the college girls came in the summer. I liked them the best, because of their wholesomeness.

I went to a cathouse once or twice a week. As a regular, I even got a cut rate. The ladies would pull my chair up the front steps and take me to a first-floor bedroom. One of the houses actually put up a ramp especially for my use; I was sort of flattered. In each house, they'd have the ladies line up in a row so I could choose which one I'd like to spend my time with. Some of the cathouses had twenty to thirty ladies on each shift. I'd only choose the ones that were able to look me in the eye. The ones I chose had to at least be friendly and receptive to the idea of sleeping with a crip.

More often than not, I'd just visit with the lady I'd selected, copping a few feels, but not actually having sex with her. But I did have some great sexual times too. The ladies of the night were a big part of my social network for several years, and they taught me lots of things about how to make love. I'm still friends with many of them.

Fantasizing

When neither external sexual expression nor masturbation is possible, a man or woman with a disability can still experience a degree of sexual fulfillment through fantasy. Whether or not it is combined with masturbation, fantasy can soothe, comfort, and make life more tolerable under even the most difficult circumstances.

When relying on fantasies to achieve sexual satisfaction alone, you can significantly increase the level of eroticism by establishing the right mood with music, scents, reading materials, or fabrics, just as you would with a partner. Creating the right atmosphere can not only enrich the experience of fantasy but make it more vivid, allowing a clearer focus on the erotic or romantic images and intensifying the pleasurable feelings that can result.

Of course, transforming sexual fantasies into a satisfying equivalent for sexual expression may not be easy. It takes practice and a profound desire to make the mind take over where the body leaves off . . . but it can be done.

Chapter 8

REPRODUCTION AND
CONTRACEPTION

*T*he majority of disabled people are capable of becoming mothers and fathers. Disability, in fact, usually has little impact on fertility. In most cases, only two questions are relevant: Is pregnancy advisable? And, if not, how can conception be avoided?

Responsible reproduction for people with disabilities may include considering genetic factors that can be passed on. While most disabling conditions are not inherited, some are, and specific probabilities can vary greatly from couple to couple. It is strongly advised that any person who believes he or she may be disabled because of hereditary factors seek out professional genetic counseling before coming to any final decision. Alternatives to traditional methods for conception have become increasingly commonplace, and these include artificial insemination, adoption, or arrangements with surrogate mothers.

Happily, many women with disabilities are capable of conceiving and bearing children. Not even a spinal cord injury with complete sensory and motor paralysis will preclude conception. However, there may be physical reasons why a woman with a disability would find pregnancy inadvisable. In some cases, pregnancy can severely compromise the health of a woman whose overall physical state is greatly affected by her disability. Each woman's situation is different, though, and only she should make these decisions. Disabled people have to right to have or not to have children, and ultimately the choice must be completely theirs.

Conception Alternatives

Men with disabilities, if they are able to ejaculate even to a limited degree, may be able to father a child. However, men with spinal cord injuries and certain other disabilities which place extreme stress on the genitourinary system may have a much lower sperm count than those who are not paralyzed. Another problem is that sometimes, even if a man can ejaculate, the ejaculate is partially expelled backward, so that much of the seminal fluid discharges into the bladder instead of being released externally.

Until the early 1970s, little research was done on the fertility of men with spinal cord injuries. But since that time many advances allow a much higher percentage of these men to father children. Most studies involved semen obtained through various artificial means.

Two medical techniques for capturing sperm have proven especially promising. The first is *electroejaculation*, in which a regulated amount of electrical current is passed to the body via probes placed in the rectum; this procedure can be painless if the spinal cord injury is complete. The current stimulates nerves which produce ejaculation, and the seminal fluid is then analyzed for sperm content. If the sperm count is low, the fluid is frozen until sperm can be added from future ejaculates. When a sufficient amount of live sperm are collected, the fluid is introduced into the partner's vagina in a process similar to artificial insemination. Many couples who had been told that conception was impossible for them have been able to become pregnant using this method.

Electroejaculation is not without certain risks, however. If the spinal cord injury is incomplete, some people may experience enough pain during the procedure to necessitate general anesthesia. Also, the electrical currents may produce a rapid rise in blood pressure. So this method is not to be undertaken without carefully consideration.

The second method is known as *high-intensity vibratory stimulation*. In this method, an especially powerful electronic vibrator is attached to the penis to produce ejaculation through stimulation of the autonomic nervous system. This method carries less risk than electroejaculation but is often not as effective.

Both methods offer potential answers to fertility problems, but neither is a complete solution. Studies have shown that 35 percent of men undergoing these treatments are able to impregnate their partners. However, some couples, even after numerous treatments, are still unable to conceive. And the procedures are not inexpensive, although insurance may cover at least part of the cost, depending on the medical plan.

There is continuing hope, however. Promising research on disabilities and fertility continues at the National Rehabilitation Hospital in Washington, D.C., the Electroejaculation and Fertility Clinic at the University of Michigan in Ann Arbor, and Craig Rehabilitation Hospital in Englewood, Colorado. (For additional organizations specializing in fertility and pregnancy issues for people with disabilities, see Appendix ■ ■)

Contraception and Disease Prevention

Just as premarital pregnancy and sexually transmitted diseases occur all too frequently among uninformed teenagers, these problems appear among many disabled individuals who are uncertain about their options for preventing conception or venereal disease. In most cases, these problems come about because people with disabilities are often deliberately infantilized by institutions or parents in a futile attempt to deemphasize their sexuality. This often leaves them uninformed about specific methods. Physicians, too, are not always aware that certain birth control methods are incompatible, and sometimes actually dangerous, for many women with disabilities.

Fortunately, awareness of and respect for the sexuality of disabled people is growing, and there has been a corresponding increase in sexual education. It is generally agreed that condoms remain the birth control and disease prevention method of choice for the nineties, since they are the only birth control method capable of preventing transmission of the AIDS virus. For people with disabilities, because of their already compromised health conditions, birth control measures may be even more important to safety and well-being than for the general population.

The simplest form of birth control (and one of the most effective when used correctly), condoms are available at most drugstores, convenience stores, and increasingly at supermarkets, bars, and gas stations. Easy to use, inexpensive, and dependable, a condom is a simple latex sheath slipped over the erect penis before intercourse. (However, sheepskin condoms *do not* prevent transmission of AIDS and other sexually transmitted diseases.)

Most of the popular brands, including Trojan, Sheik, and Ramses, now feature at least one variation that includes nonoxynol-9, a spermicidal agent which makes the condom even more effective in preventing pregnancy. It's important to remember that a condom can only be used safely with water-soluble lubricants such as K-Y jelly; an oil-based lubricant such as Vaseline or hand lotion can create holes in a condom in less than sixty seconds.

For many disabled men with urinary incontinence, the condom is already close by. Most have a supply at all times for use when connecting the penis to an external catheter for urinary drainage. Otherwise, condoms can be kept by the bed or in a nightstand, or carried in a wallet or purse.

Safer still is the use of condoms in conjunction with vaginal spermicidal foam that contains higher concentrations of nonoxynol-9, although this can cause vaginal irritation in some women. Foam can also provide vaginal lubrication when natural secretions are insufficient or absent. To be effective, a condom and/or foam must be used just before intercourse.

As with any birth control or disease control measure, there are drawbacks to these methods. Some couples find that using condoms or foam reduces their spontaneity, and others feel it interferes with male or female sensation and with oral sex. Because manual dexterity is required to insert the foam or to roll on the condom, they are not suitable for some men or for women who use catheters. This is because the condom may tear or leak as the result of the friction of sexual activity.

Other popular birth control measures include the Pill. When taken properly, the Pill is nearly 100 percent effective. However, it carries risks of side effects and adverse reactions that can be seriously damaging to the health of a disabled woman. The Pill contains powerful artificial hormones that can greatly change the ways a woman's body functions, especially with prolonged use.

The most common side effect is changes in the circulatory system, especially high blood pressure and the tendency to produce blood clots in the smaller blood vessels. This means that while a woman's disability may already have created problems with blood flow and circulation, her system may be taxed even further by these potent hormonal agents. High blood pressure and thrombophlebitis (blood clots in the vessels of the lower extremities) can pose major health risks. Women who sit in wheelchairs for long periods each day are especially vulnerable to these side effects. The Pill can also aggravate symptoms of some disabling conditions or cause depression, anxiety, or weight gain.

Another birth control possibility is a diaphragm, a rubber dome with a spring edge that covers the cervix during intercourse and is used with spermicidal jelly. A diaphragm must remain in place for eight hours after intercourse to allow the jelly to eliminate any live sperm. This device is not suitable for women with certain disabilities because good dexterity in one hand is required to insert it and to be sure it is in the proper position. Emptying the bladder by putting pressure on the abdomen, as some disabled women must do, could accidentally dislodge it. And, if the pelvic muscles are weak, there is also the potential for slippage. In addition, when sensation is lacking in the vagina, the discomfort which signals that the diaphragm is out of position or was not correctly inserted might not be felt. It is important to note that even if a woman used a diaphragm before she became disabled, she should be rechecked for proper sizing because of the loss of muscle tone and body weight that sometimes follows onset of a disability.

As with the diaphragm, foams, creams, sponges, or caps must be placed in the vagina before intercourse. This may present a problem for women whose disabilities limit their access to this part of their bodies. Some women with disabilities are able to enlist the help of a willing partner with these measures. When included in foreplay, this preparation time can even be a sensuous prelude to other eroticism.

Natural methods are the only ones we *cannot* responsibly endorse for birth control. As stated in Glorya Hale's *Sourcebook for the Disabled,*

Although natural family planning involves no medication and there are no health risks, there is a great risk of pregnancy. Even when the method is used correctly and consistently, it is only 87 percent effective. An accident, emotional distress or even moving into a new home or starting a new job can change patterns of ovulation and increase the chances of pregnancy when relying on this method. A woman with limited use of her hands might also find the necessary record-keeping, graphing and temperature taking involved in these methods difficult.

Because no known birth control method is 100 percent effective, there is always the possibility that a woman with a disability will get pregnant when she doesn't want to. Just as disabled women have the same right as nondisabled women to make decisions about their bodies, they have the right to an abortion if they choose. Despite repeated attempts to restrict the rights of women to have abortions, the procedure remains legal in the United States for every woman. The Planned Parenthood organization in your area remains the best source for information and referrals. The earlier a pregnancy is diagnosed the better; an abortion performed within the first ten weeks is generally considered a simple and safe procedure. Naturally, there is also the option of carrying a pregnancy to term and either keeping the child or offering the child up for adoption.

Permanent and semipermanent birth control options such as Norplant time-release implants are also gaining greater popularity nationwide. Vasectomy or tubal ligation is often the birth control method of choice if a couple has had all the children they want or if they prefer to remain childless. Because these procedures are usually irreversible, some physicians insist that a couple receive counseling before reaching this decision. Others will not perform either operation if they consider the patient too young or if he or she is childless. It is very important to be persistent and to seek out a sympathetic physician if this is a choice you want to pursue.

Because all methods of contraception require forethought and commitment, and because the choice will vary according to disability, it is important to seek knowledgeable counseling about birth control. The right contraceptive method can not only help avoid an unwanted pregnancy but will also enhance the intimacy and pleasure of any sexual relationship.

Chapter 9

ATTENDANTS AND SEXUAL INTIMACY

Beginning in the early 1970s, the rise of independent living centers has enabled hundreds of thousands of people with disabilities to live on their own, hold jobs, and more easily interact with the rest of society. However, independent living is not equally possible for all people who are disabled. A person with one amputated leg may, for example, be able to live a highly independent life using a regular wheelchair or a prosthesis. However, someone with quadriplegia who has complete paralysis in all four extremities, or a person with cerebral palsy in which all muscles are spastic, may only be able to live independently with the assistance of a personal care attendant. In most instances, an attendant functions as an employee; however, sometimes, because of lack of financial resources, an attendant may also be a friend or family member.

A personal care attendant is someone who, on either a paid or a volunteer basis, assists with the activities of daily living for a person who is incapable of performing these tasks on his or her own. An attendant may help with dressing, bathing, cooking, housekeeping, personal hygiene, transportation, and even such highly personal matters as intimate relations.

Ben, who has quadriplegia caused by congenital spinal muscular atrophy, uses a motorized wheelchair, has very limited use of his hands and arms, and relies on a personal aide for most daily tasks. Ben sums up his relationship with his attendant this way:

> *I have an attendant come in eight hours a day, Monday through Friday. He washes me and dresses me and drives me wherever I have to go. But romantically I'm more comfortable with the attendant out of the picture. When my girlfriend is here, the attendant goes home, leaving us our privacy.*

> *When I met my current love, I had a live-in attendant who was very instrumental in helping us establish our relationship. The first time my girlfriend and I made love, the attendant washed me and positioned me in bed so lovemaking was easy. After that, he disappeared into the other room. There were no wisecracks, no snide remarks, just good professional care. Now, when he knows my girlfriend is coming over, he arranges to leave for the evening, and I've taught my lover how to help me. It works out well.*

Others are not quite so enthusiastic and see attendant care as something they have to put up with because no alternative exists. Betsy, for example, who has quadriplegia, relies extensively on attendant care to lead a full life. She requires assistance with virtually all of her daily activities.

> *I've had many attendants. They are a necessity for social activities—but a frustration because I have to rely on them to be my arms and legs. The biggest problem is that most attendants I've*

known are not entirely dependable. It takes me a good hour and a half each morning just to get ready for the day's activities. So when my attendant is an hour or so late arriving, it messes up my entire day. And most of them are not very discreet and unobtrusive when it comes to my social relationships; they tend to make me feel like my privacy doesn't count. But I'm forced to put up with attendants to get by.

Karen is another person with a disability who finds that the issue of attendants is a double-edged sword. She uses a wheelchair because of her muscular dystrophy and relies on two shifts of attendants for daily living:

When my disabled partner and I decided to spend the night together, my nighttime attendant helps me put on my sexy nightgown and crotchless panties. Then I have to be helped into position in bed and placed with a pillow under my hips. I could tell it was difficult for the attendant to be even involved with something so intimate, and it seemed to affect the feelings of intimacy between my lover and myself.

Most respondents gave attendants mixed reviews:

I suppose it's a case of "can't live with 'em, can't live without 'em." But spontaneous lovemaking is virtually out of the question when your lives have to be timed to attendants' schedules. Having or needing them around at intimate moments is what really bugs me. Whether they're covering up their own self-consciousness or just wisecracking, the glances, comments, and sometimes outright staring are hurtful and dehumanizing. If we're going to make love, it's no business of the attendants; I think they should limit their presence to whatever is necessary or requested of them.

Despite the drawbacks, having an attendant available can make a world of difference for someone with a disability. Naturally, not every person makes a good personal aide. The most important qualifications are experience, sensitivity, and dependability. An excellent book about finding, managing, and keeping attendants is *Home Health Aids: How to Manage the People Who Help You* by Alfred DeGraff (Saratoga Access Publications). It's available from the Spinal Network Bookstore, listed under *Spinal Network Extra* in Appendix 4.

An increasingly welcome development is that many state-run and some private insurance programs are helping disabled people who lack adequate financial resources to pay for attendant care. However, these subsidies are not generally enough to provide for the level of care that is actually required for daily living, often creating considerable financial strain. Other sources of information about attendant care include the Bureau of Vocational Rehabilitation in each state and the National Council on Independent Living (see Appendix 1).

Part Two

LIVING AND LOVING WITH
SPECIFIC DISABILITIES

Chapter 10

SPINAL CORD INJURIES

*P*araplegia or quadriplegia. To most nondisabled people, these words evoke terrifying images of a living death trapped inside a useless body. But what do these terms actually mean?

Paraplegia is a type of paralysis caused by injury or disease involving the spinal cord, which is not a cord per se but a thick pathway of nerves encased in bony vertebrae. When the trauma occurs, a lesion (scar tissue) appears within the nerves of the spine. From the level of the lesion down, the muscles are paralyzed, and there is sensory loss that affects not only movement but both bladder and bowel functions.

In paraplegia, usually only the lower extremities are paralyzed, but all internal muscles and organ systems below the lesion are also affected. About half the people whose paraplegia is the result of an accident have a complete lesion, meaning that they are paralyzed on both sides of their body below the level of the injury. For the other half, the lesion is incomplete and paralysis is uneven, so that, for example, one leg may be more severely affected than the other. The *lower* the injury, the less extensive the paralysis, although even an injury in the area of the lowest sacral vertebrae (the so-called tailbone) can rob someone of the ability to walk.

Quadriplegia refers to paralysis of all four limbs. The most common causes of this type of spinal cord injury are diving accidents, falls, and traffic accidents, all situations in which the neck is traumatized. In addition to trauma, quadriplegia or other types of spinal cord dysfunction can be caused by surgery, genetic malformations, and a wide range of diseases. Whatever the cause, there is no cure for paralysis, although certain drug treatments have shown great promise if used within several hours of a paralyzing injury.

Despite significant physical limitations, people with spinal cord injuries are capable of enjoying full, active lives. Jaimie, a man with quadriplegia, is a good example. As the result of a spinal cord injury that occurred when he was pinned under a runaway tractor during his early twenties, Jaimie became completely paralyzed, experiencing total loss of sensation except in his right thumb.

Today Jaimie uses an electric wheelchair and has limited use of his arms. He is able to write, eat, and perform simple manual tasks with a brace on his right arm and drives a lift-equipped van with specially designed controls. However, he requires assistance with most aspects of daily living, and his mother serves as his full-time nurse and attendant.

After returning from the rehab hospital, Jaimie went back to college and earned his master's degree in education. Now 40, he has been teaching full-time for the past 15 years at the high school in the small town where he was born and raised.

For many years, Jaimie was reluctant to mix socially. He

had a hard time relating to others, and, while before his accident he considered himself a "real ladies' man," now he had few if any social relationships. Most people, it appeared, were extremely reluctant to include Jaimie in conversations, or so it seemed to him. Because of increasing loneliness, Jaimie began to wallow in self-pity, and most people he met started to regard him as "that poor guy who broke his neck."

Jaimie's macho pride before being injured, and his stubbornness about not encouraging people to look past his disability, did little to attract the right woman. What few relationships began quickly fizzled, and Jaimie eventually gave up completely on finding the right person. But then, as he recounts,

> I met Marlina through a friend at school. She seemed to draw out of me the renewed desire to have a relationship with a woman. She sensed my reluctance to get involved and knew the reasons I felt the way I did. But it didn't seem to faze her at all. In the first several months I knew her, we talked a lot, for hours at a time, about our lives and aspirations. She taught me how to strive for better things in life, sometimes in the face of overwhelming obstacles. Her life had seen its own share of tragedy and what seemed to be insurmountable barriers. But she overcame them, and she convinced me that I could too. If it's one thing Marlina really showed me how to do it's try.

> Of course, we fell in love. I guess that inevitably happens when a man and a woman spend a lot of time together and become as close as we were. We became totally inseparable and spent almost all our spare time together. Even my mother came to love Marlina, thank God, giving our relationship her full approval. I guess Mom was sort of relieved that her son was finally getting back to a normal life after all these years.

> Marlina was also able to reawaken my long dormant sexuality. It seemed a relief to once again have the feelings that I'd known before

83

my injury. I'd thought that I'd never feel that way toward a woman again. So I quit trying to. The doctors, counselors, and everybody else had said either directly or indirectly that there were more important things in life than sex. Like what, I always wondered?

In time Marlina and I became intimate sexually. This was really a big surprise to me because I was not sure I was physically capable of pleasing a woman sexually, nor did I ever expect any woman would want me that way again. But with Marlina's help and cooperation, we were able to satisfy one another's sexual needs. No, it's not the same as before I became paralyzed, but it's sex just the same. We make love differently than others, but who's to say what's normal?

One of our biggest problems is that it takes two people to get me transferred from my wheelchair into bed or vice versa. So that necessitates having another person present whenever we have sex. Although Marlina has taught me to try new and different methods of doing all kinds of things, this is one area where I've drawn the line and stood fast. So, for the most part, we have sex with me remaining in my chair. This calls for quite a bit of agility on Marlina's part, but as long as she's willing and able, so am I.

Although I have no feeling, I can get erections, quite satisfactory ones, as a matter of fact. So Marlina and I have intercourse in the usual way, with her straddling me in the seated positions. I keep my catheter and leg bag on during sex, just folding it back along my penis. Marlina says she doesn't even notice the catheter during intercourse. For me the most pleasant and stimulating sex is of the oral variety, with me going down on Marlina while keeping my right thumb inside her vagina. I still have feeling in that thumb, and the friction and squeezes that I feel as she and I make love wildly excite me. As amazing as it sounds, my thumb has become my sex organ.

Although I'm unable to ejaculate, the stimulation that I'm able to feel with my thumb, mouth, and tongue is incredibly powerful. The result is something indescribable that amounts to a kind of orgasm. It's not what nondisabled people might feel, but it's just as good, only in a different kind of way. More than just the sex, it's the combination of intimacy and words, the total sharing that makes our lovemaking such a satisfying experience.

We live in a small town, and often when I'm at Marlina's place with my van parked on the street in front, some of my students will drive by and "toot" us, just to let me know they're aware of what's going on. This and their teasing comments at school used to annoy me somewhat, but I've gotten used to it, and so have they. Most people in town, including my students, recognize us as a couple. I think marriage is a definite possibility for us.

Ellen Stohl, a woman with quadriplegia resulting from an automobile accident, represents the other end of the spectrum. Because her injury involves a partial lesion of the spinal cord, Ellen has retained sensation in her genitals, despite the fact that many of her muscles are paralyzed and some areas of her body are insensitive to heat, cold, or touch.

Since appearing in *Playboy* in a pictorial, Ellen has become an ombudsperson for the sexual rights of the disabled. She is very direct in discussing how her disability has affected her sexuality:

I'm an adventurous sort, but being disabled is a strong deterrent to spontaneity. For bladder control, I need to wear protective undergarments, which make me feel about as sexy as a toad. Also, since I am supersensitive in the genital area, the feeling of impending orgasm is much like the sensation of having to pee. So often, when I'm close to climaxing, I almost stop myself. I've read studies that show this feeling is common in many women, but no one ever discusses it. These embarrassing fears tend to limit my sexual activity to my own home or a place where there's a bathroom that's wheelchair accessible. Sex on the beach, in a car, or a quickie at the office are just not in my repertoire.

The best sex comes from open communication and the willingness to be silly, to forget about the inconveniences the disability creates. I'm always open about my disability and willing to talk about it. I always empty my bladder before sex and make sure we're in a place where both of us are comfortable. I've read a lot of books on sex and sexuality, so I've been able to develop my own sexual techniques that I've tailored to my abilities. Sometimes, I even try things I don't think I can do because maybe, just maybe, there's a variation that will work for me. I'm willing to experiment, and so far I've heard few complaints.

The key to my sexual contentment is being honest with the person I'm with and feeling comfortable with the surroundings I'm in. Whenever I'm uncomfortable, I talk about it. Sex is not just an activity, it's the most intimate form of communication. Above all, you've got to be sure to communicate freely.

Frank was 48 years old when he became paralyzed, the result of an error during surgery to repair his blocked aorta. The blood supply to his spinal cord was restricted, resulting in damage to the spinal cord. Frank has paraplegia, with complete paralysis beginning at the level of his navel.

Just five months after he became disabled, Frank's life was shattered when his wife of twenty-five years passed away. Adding to his problems, he was no longer able to keep his job in institutional management, despite having more than two decades of seniority. His employer retired him on a pension of two-thirds his former salary.

The physical manifestations of his disability left Frank unable to experience erections or to feel any sensation below waist level. However, he remained very strong in his upper body and had normal sensation in all areas unaffected by the paralysis. At first, Frank's lack of genital functioning troubled him greatly. This, coupled with the untimely loss of his wife, plunged him into a depression that lasted about a year.

After this period, Frank met Lea, the woman who was to

become his second wife. At the time, many people said that a woman of 40 who wanted to be married to a man in a wheelchair "had to have a few screws loose." Of course, that bothered both of them greatly. But it also served as incentive to try to create a successful intimate relationship:

The chemistry was just there between us. She understands me and my physical problems. And the fact that I'm paralyzed doesn't seem to bother her all that much. Lea is a wonderful person, beautiful both inside and out. I wonder if I would have cared to continue living much longer had we not met.

My new marriage has taught me that the fears I had about my manhood and sexuality as a disabled person were empty ones. Although I miss the conventional sex most men and women experience, I've learned to cherish what I still have. We may make love differently, but it's just as rewarding, just as satisfying, and just as meaningful to us as a couple.

Since I can't have erections, manual stimulation and oral sex are my only alternatives. This has not really affected my sex life much, just the way in which I make love. Prior to meeting me, Lea was not attuned to oral sex at all. However, we discussed my physical problems openly and agreed to experiment with various sexual alternatives. She now says that the experiences she has had with our lovemaking are as satisfying as any she has ever experienced.

One of the reasons Lea and I get along so well, not only sexually but in every area of married life, is that she has a 21-year-old son who is also in a wheelchair. He's a quad, the result of radiation treatments for cancer. I feel that Lea was more receptive to a relationship with me due to her familiarity with people with disabilities. Her son has been disabled for five years, and all three of us are active in the disability rights movement in our community.

Betsy, a woman with quadriplegia from a congenital disability known as spinal muscular atrophy, also weathered her share of romantic storms before finding the right partner. Betsy has no muscular control in her legs and very limited use of her arms and hands. She uses an electric wheelchair and needs assistance with most daily activities.

Until she was 29, Betsy lived at home with her parents. It was a poor arrangement for her, she says, and the architectural barriers, lack of readily accessible transportation, and smothering overprotectiveness of her mother and father added to her misery. Betsy feels she was brainwashed by parental attitudes and media images into believing that as a disabled person she was romantically unacceptable. As a result, she struggled with poor self-esteem for many years.

Finally, Betsy became involved in an independent living program which enabled her to move into her own apartment and hire paid attendants. But her romantic life didn't change as dramatically—or as quickly—as she had hoped:

Men still reacted to my disability mostly with discomfort, at least until they got to know me. Some pitied me, some were in awe of my "bravery," and many treated me like a child. For these reasons, most of the men I expressed a romantic interest in didn't return my feelings. It was incredibly frustrating.

Once, before I got my apartment, one guy was interested, but I was acting like I was too sheltered for him (probably true), and the relationship never really got off the ground. Another man (also disabled) saw me as his only hope for romance, and that didn't work either. Then, finally, I met a man who considered me a sexually attractive woman.

That was David, the man who is now my husband. We've been married almost two years now. David is also disabled, a paraplegic. I never really thought I'd fall in love with another disabled person, but that's what happened. David is the world's most loving person. He's probably more understanding about my disability because he's in a wheelchair himself. But I've always thought that David would be the way he is even if he was not disabled. That's just the way he is—warm, compassionate, and understanding.

One of the first things that crosses people's minds when they see us together is How in the world do they make love? The answer is: Very well, thank you.

David is the only man I've ever had a sexual relationship with. We're so good for each other. We communicate freely and love each other very deeply. And we are each other's best friends. I can imagine how people must see us as the perfect match of sexual nothingness. After all, both of us are paralyzed. We can't feel sex the way other people do. David has problems sometimes getting an erection. And when we do have intercourse, we don't really feel it. I'm sure people are thinking, So why bother?

But it's not that way at all. David and I have a great sex life. It's fantastic, the togetherness, the intimacies, the kissing, the stimulation we're still able to receive despite our paralysis. Maybe if either of us wasn't disabled we'd be able to do more exciting things physically, like using a greater variety of positions, or making love in places that aren't accessible to us.

But to us, both of our bodies are beautiful and exciting. And when we make love, we move together into a sexual rhythm and climax in a way that satisfies us both. After all, who else is there that matters? We tell each other exactly what we like and what we want to do, and then we just do it. Communication is especially important to us since I can't move much, and David has to help me do all the things I want to do.

Sometimes we talk about our sex fantasies, acting out what we can and otherwise just describing them to each other while holding, kissing, and caressing. We're not afraid to experiment with sex, because we've found that if we don't try it, there's no way of knowing what's best for us.

Betsy and David's commitment to each other has grown into a professional partnership as well. Together they have designed and are building a bed and breakfast inn specifically for guests with disabilities. "Beyond the elimination of architectural and natural barriers, we hope the inn will address attitudinal barriers as well," David says. "All too often, people with a disability are overpatronized, ignored, stared at, asked embarrassing personal questions, or treated like children. In a business run by disabled for disabled, these attitudes will simply not exist. Betsy's and my goal is to provide total accessibility by giving our guests their independence. By catering primarily to the disabled, we will eliminate the anxiety of being treated like a 'disabled person' instead of just a person."

As Betsy and David have discovered, a loving, determined couple, regardless of the disability of one or both partners, can find ways to fulfill their sexual needs and offer each other maximum satisfaction.

Additional information on spinal cord injuries and other types of paralysis is available through the following organizations and resources:

American Paralysis Association
500 Morris Avenue
Springfield, NJ 07081
(800) 526-3456
(201) 379-2690

National Head Injury Foundation
333 Turnpike Road
Southborough, MA 01772
(508) 485-9950

National Spinal Cord Injury Association
600 West Cummings Park, Suite 2000

Woburn, MA 01801
(800) 962-9629
(617) 935-2722

Paralyzed Veterans of America
801 Eighteenth Street, NW
Washington, DC 20006
(202) 872-1300

Handbook on Sexuality After Spinal Cord Injury. Full of valuable exercises to develop sexual/sensual awareness and written with a refreshing sense of humor, this book is available from Craig Rehabilitation Hospital.

The Sensuous Wheeler: Sexual Adjustment for the Spinal Cord Injured, by Barry Jo Rabin (self published in Long Beach, California). Although this well-written book is for those with spinal cord injuries, any person with a disability can gain from it insight into his or her sexuality.

Sexual Adjustment: A Guide for the Spinal Cord Injured, by Martha Ferguson Gregory (Bloomington, Ill.: Cheever Publishing, Accent Special Publications, 1974). Written by a vocational rehabilitation counselor married to a man with paraplegia, this is a practical, down-to-earth guide to the sexual adjustments required by a spinal cord injury.

Sexual Options for Paraplegics and Quadriplegics, by Thomas O. Mooney, Theodore M. Cole, and Richard A. Chilgren (Boston: Little, Brown, 1975). This clearly written book for people with spinal cord injuries and their partners has a wealth of specific how-to information. Written by a spinal cord–injured person, with the assistance of two physicians experienced in human sexuality research and rehabilitation, it includes photos showing spinal cord–injured people preparing for and participating in various kinds of sexual expression, with special attention to the problems of people who must wear catheters or ileostomy bags and those who cannot move their arms, legs, or both.

Sexuality and the Spinal Cord Injured Woman, by Sue Bregman (Minneapolis: Sister Kenny Institute, 1975). This book offers straightforward advice on social and sexual adjustment and counters stereotyped attitudes toward the sexual potential of women with spinal injuries.

POLIO AND POSTPOLIO SYNDROME

P robably the best-known neurological disability other than spinal cord injury is polio, short for poliomyelitis. A viral disease which affects the anterior nerve cells of the spinal cord and brain stem and can cause complete or partial muscular paralysis, polio has been virtually eliminated worldwide since development of the Salk and Sabin vaccines in the 1950s.

However, many thousands of people who were disabled by polio still wrestle with its aftermath, including breathing difficulties caused by the initial bout of the disease and the lingering, energy-draining effects of postpolio syndrome. They may have to rely on a respirator to breathe. Yet, unlike someone who is disabled by a spinal cord injury, a person who has had polio has complete physical feeling. Sensation, including sexual functioning, is generally not affected.

Marilyn is an example of a woman who feels she has had to fight an unending battle to be accepted by men since she contracted polio:

> *Right after becoming disabled, I discovered that people, especially men, reacted differently to me in many ways. There's a lot of avoidance, "shutting me out" of things, seeing me and quickly looking the other way, which never gives me the chance to establish eye contact, smile, or begin to speak. Men, especially single men, seem to be especially ill at ease. They act nervous, uncomfortable, and frightened, all of which does my female ego no good at all. Men rarely flirt or ask for my phone number (or, God forbid, a date!). Some differences are so subtle that I can barely tell if they're really happening. But I know it all boils down to one thing: I'm treated differently.*

> *Not long after becoming disabled, I became aware that most people assume I no longer have feeling in my legs (I do), am not able to have sex (I can), cannot have an orgasm (I can), and that I cannot have sexual relationships. This seems to be the most pervasive and common stereotype—the myth of the "sexless cripple."*

> *My sexuality is a part of me. Disability doesn't change it at all. In the thirty years I've been disabled, I've had relationships with a number of men, and there have also been times when I've gone without a man, not even a date, for a long period of time. Right now I've been dateless for more than three years, without any type of relationship, and sometimes the loneliness is unbearable. But I keep looking, because I know that sooner or later I will meet the right someone again. This is an area of life that's important enough that there's no way I can just simply give up. Even though I sometimes feel I should give up, I won't.*

Despite her current "dry spell," Marilyn was able to enjoy a satisfying sex life in the past.

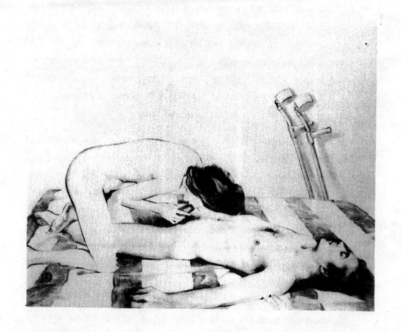

I don't really use any special techniques when I have sex. I've found I can use a number of positions, and often do. I've had intercourse with my legs apart (missionary style) or together with my knees against my chest, with my lover in front or behind me as I lie on my side; with me on my stomach as the man enters from behind; and with me on top sort of lying forward on his chest. I've also used one other position that is difficult to describe but offers a great degree of comfort and the opportunity for mutual stimulation. This position involves me lying on my back with my legs up and draped over my partner, who is lying on his side and enters me at a 45-degree angle; the position is very restful and allows us to make love for long periods without tiring.

In most positions, it's better for me if my lover is able to hold me by the buttocks and raise my hips. This increases the effectiveness of his movements and also gives him better access to my vagina. It's often possible to switch positions without breaking apart if he's careful to move slowly and hold my buttocks firmly against him. If the position calls for it, I can keep my legs up high by holding them with my hands hooked under the knees. If my arms get tired, I may hook my ankles on my partner's shoulders, which requires minimal effort on my part (although I don't recommend this with a man who has a longer than average penis—penetration can be too deep and painful). Or, with my partner over me, if I want to hold my legs closer together, I can have him position his ankles over mine for extra support.

I think it's experimenting that's important, seeing what works and what doesn't, keeping an open mind and not being overly self-conscious or inflexible, and not taking every little thing too seriously. Sex is supposed to be fun. That's what I try to remember most.

Being severely disabled can sometimes result in humorous predicaments. Marilyn describes a date some years ago with Phillip, a man she had been seeing for several months:

Phillip had always been very understanding about my disability, always willing to give me whatever assistance I needed ... without ever making a big fuss over it. But once we ran into a situation which to us, at least, was absolutely hilarious.

Since I have difficulties in transferring in and out of my wheelchair without assistance, I've trained myself to go to the bathroom just three times a day when I know assistance will be available (usually in the form of my attendant). I urinate at 7:00 A.M., 2:00 P.M., and 10:00 P.M. I have terrific bladder control, and usually, if I watch my fluid intake, I have no trouble keeping on schedule.

One evening Phillip and I went to dinner at this nice restaurant. After drinking a bit too much liquid, I discovered I had an urgent need to stop at the ladies' room. Naturally, as luck would have it, no one was around to help me except Phillip. Our dilemma was— and this is something that has never been covered by Amy Vanderbilt or Emily Post—do we use the men's room or the ladies' room? After a quick discussion, we decided to use the ladies' room. Phillip and I had already been intimate, so it was not a question of either of us being embarrassed. I had a waitress check to make sure the facilities were not being used and asked her to "stand guard" while Phillip and I were in there. But, evidently, she had to leave her post for a phone call.

Phillip stood me up in the last stall against the wall (a standing pivot transfer) and had one hand under my dress getting ready to reach for my panties. Suddenly, we heard someone else in the bathroom. The door to our stall was wide open, but this woman didn't seem to notice. She entered one of the other stalls, proceed to go, and then afterwards walked over to the sink. Phillip and I had been, to that point, stone silent. Then I giggled, and she looked up and saw us both in the mirror.

She shrieked and then ran out the ladies' room door screaming, "My God, there's a man in there dancing with a woman." I don't think she even noticed the wheelchair or our compromising posi-

tion.

I guess it could have been worse. I often wonder what the woman would have said if she'd seen Phillip pulling down my panties with my dress hoisted to my waist! "My God, there's a man and a woman in there . . ." Well, you can guess the rest.

Despite the fact that sexual function is left intact, polio inflicts tremendous damage on the muscular and respiratory system and can sometimes result in death from breathing difficulties.

Every day, Lois, now age 62, gives thanks that she was one of the fortunate ones. When Louis was about to graduate from grade school, she awoke one morning with a high fever, nausea, and an unusually stiff neck. Her mother called the family doctor, who diagnosed pneumonia and had her admitted to a local hospital. Lois's health continued to decline, and, after a few days, she developed weakness in all four limbs, difficulty breathing, and sharp pains when inhaling.

Lois turned out to have a case of polio that brought her close to death several times. Fortunately, she recovered. Today she is in good health and in good spirits, except when her postpolio syndrome saps her strength and endurance.

Although she has not had any serious romantic involvements for more than ten years, Lois does not seem to miss having one at the moment. She is content to live out the remainder of her life as a single person, concentrating on her career, her family, and her community activities.

I've been disabled for a long time, more than half a century. For the most part, though, I've been able to do quite well. I drive—always have—even back in the days before cars had automatic transmissions. I can negotiate most steps, and I usually walk, since I feel that using the wheelchair is not good for me. Walking on crutches helps me maintain good muscle tone.

I've had no serious problems in maintaining social and romantic relationships that I can trace back to my disability. I've had many men friends and a number of romantic relationships, including two marriages and a live-together situation. My romantic partners seem to have been able to accept my disability once we were involved, but I have no doubt that my disability probably prevented a lot of men from becoming involved with me in the first place. Some of my first husband's friends asked him, "She's got brains, but why in the world did you marry her?" It's difficult for some people to understand that a disability doesn't matter when it comes to the quality and satisfaction of a close relationship.

Though none of my romantic relationships ended due to my disability, I feel that it may have been a large factor in the instability of some of my love affairs. I've always suffered from insecurities about my own sexuality as it relates to my disability. This often led to romantic entanglements that were not as solid as they should have been. Because of self-doubts over my ability to be sexually desirable, I often felt threatened by the prospect of losing a lover to someone more sexually competent and desirable. These feelings would often lead me to being insanely jealous, and at times I would drink heavily.

Most of my negative feelings of sexual inferiority came from the fact that I always thought I would be unable to make sex enjoyable enough for my partner. I felt that my not being able to move about more freely and use my pelvic muscles made it impossible for me to keep a man happy sexually. Although I "performed" in bed as best as I could, this insecurity was always at the back of my mind.

To make matters worse, I never shared my doubts about my sexuality with any of my partners. We never talked about sex, how to make it better or what ways we could use to please each other more. I never discussed how my needs and sexual abilities might be different because I was disabled. We just did it. Had sex. You know . . . the old "to have and to hold, for better or for worse" thing.

Sure enough, with each successive relationship, things got worse.

But my problems never appeared to be related to sex, at least not on the surface. Years later, after much soul-searching, I came to realize that most of my romantic failures came from the latent doubts I had about myself as a disabled person, and the fears I had about my own sexuality.

I now know that much of this could have been prevented by communicating, talking and discussing my feelings and fears with my partners. There must have been ways to dispel my feelings of being so damn inadequate as a woman. But since we never discussed it, we never came up with any answers.

If I had it to do over again, I think I'd do it differently. Intimacy means communicating. Without exchanging ideas and concerns, any relationship is going to fail.

Unlike Lois, who had difficulty coming to terms with her sexuality as a disabled person, Donna's story shows that just the opposite can also hold true. Although Donna was disabled by the aftermath of polio, she feels she has been able to enjoy a fulfilling life.

Donna was born with congenital subvalvular aortic stenosis, a heart condition that causes circulatory problems and general weakness. Then, to compound her problems, Donna became ill with polio, which left her unable to walk and with only limited strength in her upper body. She became wholly dependent on care from her parents. Donna underwent several major operations as a child to correct her heart problems, and several more to correct the physical conditions caused by the polio. Today she can walk with braces and crutches, but she still tires easily and spends most of her time in a wheelchair.

Although she is currently on a daily regimen of muscle relaxants and antiinflammatory drugs to manage the pain in her bones and joints, Donna remains upbeat and optimistic:

Sure, life with a disability is no pleasure—if you let it be that way. I sure don't!

Having been disabled my entire life, I've learned that I'm really no different than anyone else. Maybe I do things, physical things, a bit differently, but I want the same things from life that everyone else wants. And I'm happy, extremely happy.

I've been married to the same wonderful man for more than seventeen years, and we have two teenage children. We also have a nice home with an all-American mortgage, car payments every month, a dog and two cats, and all the pleasures and heartaches of any other family, I suppose.

Though I still have problems physically, I've had professional counseling that has helped me tremendously in finding out who I am, what I am, and what I want out of life. Occasionally, I still experience episodes of anger and sadness over my disability, but for the most part I think I am pretty happy.

Until a few months ago, I'd worked for over twenty years as a legal assistant, but my employer had to let me go because I had to cut back on my hours due to increasing fatigue from postpolio syndrome. I was angry at first, then sad and full of self-pity for a while. Now I've accepted the fact that my disability has caught up to me, and I'm thankful for the years in which I was able to function unaffected by it.

My husband and I have enjoyed a wonderful relationship throughout our marriage. I think that's because we care for each other so much that we're both always willing to talk about our problems. We do what pleases the other.

We've had a pretty good sex life, too. About the only difficulty we've had lately is when I'm over tired, which is unfortunately more and more often. But with an understanding mate, even these difficulties can be minor ones. We talk about things, find solutions, and everything is okay.

We work at trying not to lose the romance in our relationship, which is very easy to do when you're focused on physical problems.

I try to reinforce my own sexuality with a positive mental attitude. I wear sexy lingerie for my husband, tell him about my sexual fantasies, and we always express in words what we like and appreciate about each other, sexually and otherwise. I think we've achieved true mutual happiness and sexual fulfillment.

Additional information on polio and postpolio syndrome is available through the following organizations and resources:

National Easter Seal Society
70 East Lake Street
Chicago, IL 60601
(312) 726-6200

Sister Kenny Institute
Chicago Avenue at Twenty-seventh Street
Minneapolis, MN 55407
(612) 863-4457

No Apologies: A Survival Guide and Handbook for the Disabled Written by the Real Authorities—People with Disabilities and Their Families, by Florence Weiner (New York: St. Martin's Press, 1986). This is a wonderful collection of essays and resources. Several of the essays are written by men and women with polio and postpolio syndrome.

Toward Intimacy—Family Planning and Sexuality Concerns of Physically Disabled Women, by the Task Force on Concerns of Physically Disabled Women (New York: Human Sciences Press, 1978). Not just about the effects of polio, this book offers a comprehensive approach to the problems of all women with disabilities. It is upbeat, supportive, and informative.

Chapter 12

MULTIPLE SCLEROSIS

*M*ultiple sclerosis (or MS) is one of the most common organic diseases affecting the nervous system. It usually strikes young adults between the ages of 20 and 35. This devastating disease affects many parts of the nervous system and is often characterized by relapses followed by remissions of partial and, occasionally, complete recovery. Multiple sclerosis involves the nerves of the spinal cord, causing periods of partial to complete paralysis of the legs and, at times, the trunk and arms. Numbness, tingling, and sensory changes are also very common.

The disease's name stems from the scar (sclerotic) tissue which forms on the myelin sheath covering nerve fibers of the brain and spinal cord, weakening the nerve impulses. If the nerve fibers themselves are destroyed, impulses can no longer be carried to various parts of the body and muscle function cannot be restored. The basic causes of multiple sclerosis are still undiscovered.

Sexually, most people with MS experience only transient difficulties, especially in the early stages of the disease. Men may have occasional episodes of impotence, but, except in those with advanced stages of MS, inability to achieve and maintain an erection is only a temporary problem. Some women with MS suffer from anesthesia or numbness in the genital area that prevents them from experiencing sexual pleasure to the degree they'd want to. This is usually transient, however, and women often report that they are able to use other methods of achieving sexual satisfaction similar to those used by women with spinal cord injuries.

Bonnie is a 37-year-old woman who first showed signs of MS eight years ago. She has the chronic form of the disease, which has a rapid, unexpected onset and progresses quickly to become a severe disability. Her first symptoms were lack of coordination when trying to walk and periods of alternating hot flashes and chills.

Within a year, Bonnie was unable to walk at all and barely able to stand. Her legs would often buckle under her without warning. Today Bonnie can still walk with a walker, but, after about twenty feet, she becomes overwhelmed by fatigue. She uses a wheelchair most of the time and drives a car equipped with hand controls. Her arms are somewhat uncoordinated, and she tires easily, so her time behind the wheel is limited.

Mentally, Bonnie is extremely sharp and a self-admitted workaholic and compulsive volunteer. She says that her brain can always find six ways to do four things. However, her body frustrates her by not being able to keep up.

I feel lucky that when I got MS I had already been married to Mark for several years. Of course, finding out that I had a chronic, incurable disability was hard on both of us. I'll admit there have been times when MS has strained our relationship to close to its breaking point. But Mark still loves me, although he hates the disease. That makes two of us.

Difficult as it's been, we've managed to overcome the problems of MS and still love each other very much. We've tried to keep the romance alive in our relationship and decided long ago (even before MS) that we'd never left the flame of love die out. Mark is an understanding husband who has helped me very much, especially in the first few years of my disability, when I desperately fought against what I perceived to be the injustice of my condition.

At first I was angry about being disabled and found it hard to cope with the changes and limitations it created in my life. My bitterness became all-encompassing, and for a while my self-pity threatened the stability of our marriage. Mark wouldn't let me drag our relationship down, though, and he showed me how to fight it and live a happy life despite being disabled. I owe much of this attitude change to Mark, who stuck by me even during those times when I'd given up on myself.

Mark has always been my lover and best friend. He's a man who's willing to put up with all the crap MS has handed us, just because he loves me. Even when I hit bottom trying to adjust to my new disability, Mark was always somehow able to make me feel like a desirable woman and an equal partner in life.

The limitations Bonnie's disability imposed on her and Mark's sex life initially took some getting used to.

Since the MS has produced a sort of mild anesthesia in my genital area (I don't have complete sensation there), I need direct clitoral stimulation in order to have an orgasm. Mark and I use different techniques to do this. Either I lie on my back with Mark on his side stroking me, or we use a position with me on my back and my legs draped over his while he sits facing me.

We've discovered the benefits of using a vibrator (both internally

*and externally) to give me the immense amount of stimulation I
need without either of us getting tired. This gives me orgasms—
still inspired by Mark—and pleases both of us very much. Mark
and I have come to a sexual understanding, too, that during some
of the times when I'm just too tired for intercourse, it's perfectly
acceptable for me to stroke him to orgasm and give him a hand job.
This is great for when I want to express my love for him but just
feel beat energy-wise. We've found the vibrator also works on him
too.*

Unlike Bonnie, whose energy is severely taxed by the
disease, some people with MS retain their stamina, although
they may grapple with other physical limitations. Sharon is a
37-year-old woman who has had MS for sixteen years. Her
disability creates ataxia (a lack of coordination) as well as spasticity in her legs and tremors in her hands and arms. She is able
to stand, provided she leans against a solid object, but is unable
to walk without support. The majority of the time, Sharon uses
a wheelchair.

In addition to walking difficulties, Sharon's MS causes
unpredictable vision disturbances, including blurred vision and
haziness, and she wears thick corrective lenses for reading. She
calls herself a slow mover, having to make major movements
carefully. If she tries to hurry through any task, her spasticity
makes it virtually impossible.

Sharon had been married one year when she was diagnosed with MS. Her marriage lasted ten years and ended in
divorce for reasons largely unrelated to her disability. Sharon is
totally independent, lives alone, and genuinely enjoys her life.
In the six years since her divorce, she feels she has blossomed
both as a person and as a woman.

*I've really spread my wings since becoming single again. It's not
been easy being disabled. But I adore my independence and self-
sufficiency. Every day is a gift accepted with joy. Even in pain,
there is a life and it is mine!*

Sharon has had about a dozen romantic relationships since her divorce. The best, she says, have been with disabled men. Her latest relationship is with a man who has quadriplegia.

I've been involved for about a year with a man who is brilliant, funny, good-looking, sexy, a good friend, talented co-worker, and a fantastic lover. He's also disabled by a "double whammy"; he became a paraplegic from a spinal cord injury in 1969 and a quad in 1972 when he broke his neck in an auto accident. We'd known each other for more than three years before our flirting progressed to a full-fledged love affair.

This man has reawakened my sexual self beyond my wildest imagination. Though I responded to him hesitantly, I've also had to allow myself to relinquish my control and trust him. This has been most difficult for me, to really risk myself completely in an intimate relationship. Most of my previous relationships have been purely physical, which was by choice. This relationship has gone beyond sexual infatuation. I think it's a little frightening for both of us, frankly. But being in love is also very exhilarating. We've both been badly burned before, and I don't know who's warier. I'm ready for a commitment, I think, but I'm very self-protective.

Our sex life is spectacular! I only wish I were more physically able, in terms of strength and balance, to offer more variety to my disabled partner. I'm definitely multiorgasmic with him—it's great.

Being in my thirties and having had half a dozen lovers ranging from great to incredible has really opened up my sex life. I had doubts about my disability hampering me. And the big message that I got, from doctors, friends, and everybody, said that since I was disabled I might as well forget about physical pleasure for myself and concentrate on giving pleasure to my partner. Thank God a disability has nothing to do with sexual satisfaction. It will if you let it, but in most cases that's not the way it has to be.

Oral sex is my favorite sexual technique. It's less physically demanding and, for me, very satisfying. Masturbation, either alone or for or with my lover, has also been a terrific lesson in sexuality. And it's taught me to be more sexually assertive and to better understand my own body. I also love realistic dildos and vibrators. All of these, alone or in combination, can make for a great sex life, whether or not regular intercourse is possible. And being disabled really doesn't have much to do with it.

My advice is to always have a positive sexual outlook. Love yourself, and it will shine through to make others love you.

Additional information on multiple sclerosis is available through the following organizations:

ATOMS (Association to Overcome Multiple Sclerosis)
79 Milk Street
Boston, MA 02109

National Multiple Sclerosis Society
205 East Forty-second Street
New York, NY 10017
(800) 624-8236
(212) 986-3240
Publishes *MS Keynotes* and *MS Messenger.*

$\boxed{\textit{Chapter 13}}$

MUSCULAR DYSTROPHY
AND OTHER
NEUROMUSCULAR
DISABILITIES

*M*uscular dystrophy (MD) is actually not one disease but many. It is a group of hereditary diseases characterized by progressive weakening and degeneration of the muscles, resulting from a genetic defect in metabolism.

Of the three main types of MD, pseudohypertrophic (Duchenne) is the most common and the most severe. It occurs only in males, sometimes at birth, but usually between the ages of two and six, with rapid progression and no remission. It starts with the muscles of the pelvic area, a waddling gait, and difficulty climbing stairs and rising from the floor, then spreads to the shoulders and other parts of the body.

The Landouzy-Déjerine type, probably the most benign, usually appears in late adolescence. It affects the face and shoulder muscles first and sometimes progresses very slowly, with plateaus of significant duration and with minimal disability.

Myotonic dystrophy strikes in young adulthood and, unlike the other types, affects the muscles of the extremities first, with disability progressing steadily and becoming very severe within fifteen to twenty years.

People with MD usually have complete tactile perceptions and full use of their senses. The disease attacks only the motor muscles, although in rare instances cardiac and respiratory functions can also be impaired. Because the disease is transmitted through male genes, MD is much more prevalent in men. The hereditary connection is clear, and many families have two or more offspring with MD. Unfortunately, there is no known cure.

Most people with MD eventually need a wheelchair. At this stage, the person with the disease will also become unable to perform most tasks requiring physical effort, and some assistance with dressing and day-to-day activities may be necessary.

Jim has had muscular dystrophy since infancy. His muscles deteriorated rapidly, and the disease progressed throughout his grade school years. By the time he was a teenager, he was using a wheelchair, and today, at age 36, he gets around in a power wheelchair he controls with a mouth stick. A specially outfitted computer helps him write the same way.

Jim's top priority right now is to enjoy a meaningful relationship with a woman. Throughout his life, he has had friendship-only relationships. Although he's been infatuated with several women, he has never been in a mutually caring relationship, nor has he ever had sex. His only sexual outlets are fantasizing and masturbating. Even masturbating is sometimes extremely difficult because of Jim's lack of strength, and he is frequently unable to have an orgasm.

Although I've been attracted to many women, none have felt strongly enough about me to meet me halfway. I find this acutely frustrating. Inside this disabled body is a highly sexual creature who yearns for ways to express what he feels. But it's almost impossible with the kind of disability I have. And I understand why women have a tough time relating to me as a sexual partner. Physically, I'm totally dependent; I probably couldn't be very active in sex anyway. Yet I've given it a lot of thought, and I know I could still express myself sexually.

I have no trouble maintaining an erection. And I know I could perform oral sex if need be. I've got it all planned out in my mind, if and when it ever happens. It's just that it's so incredibly difficult finding the right partner. Oh, there are lots of women I've met that love to talk and flirt, but as soon as we start into anything romantic or intimate, things end quickly.

I used to be quite shy about meeting women. Now, as I'm older, I've learned to be a lot better at striking up a conversation and being interesting. I think I'm a lot of fun to be with, and so do lots of my friends. Women are attracted to me, but not yet as a romantic partner. But I've never lost my faith. I take one day at a time and focus on my dreams and aspirations. I really believe that, someday, the right woman will come along. Life holds many surprises.

Irene, too, has endured countless rejections because of her MD. She was born with a rare form of the disease that causes breathing difficulties. Although it was apparent at birth that something was wrong, doctors were unable to pinpoint the problem until Irene was about six months of age and had difficulty sitting up on her own. When her parents placed her in a sitting position, she'd fall over, her torso virtually caving in from lack of muscle tone. As a result of her disease, Irene has severe scoliosis, a curvature of the spine to one side which causes her internal organs to be compressed, so her lungs don't have enough room to expand.

Over the years, Irene's spinal deformity has left her unable to breathe on her own. She now has a permanent tracheostomy (a plastic tube surgically implanted in the windpipe below the voice box) to reduce the amount of air she needs to breathe with each respiration. The breathing tube protrudes from her neck and provides an open passageway so air can reach her lungs directly—without traveling through her nose or mouth.

Irene spends several hours each day on a respirator, which allows her to conserve whatever energy she has for other activities. At night, the respirator does all her breathing for her.

I'm now 38 years old and have been disabled my entire life. When I was younger, I had a bit of a problem meeting people; I guess they were put off by my physical problems. My slouch because of my spinal curvature didn't help much. I dated a little bit back in high school, but nothing ever really serious. Then, at age 22, I met Doyle.

We fell in love and married a few months later. He is the most wonderful, understanding man I have ever met. I told Doyle when we first got together there was a possibility I couldn't have children, but he took it in stride. And the disability didn't put him off like it did other men. He says he was attracted to me for my personality and who I was as a human being.

We had, of course, explored the possibilities of having children. But my doctors advised against it. When I was 25, I took my doctors' advice and had a tubal ligation. Doyle and I had been worried about playing "Russian roulette" with my health after several doctors advised us that I might die if I became pregnant.

A few years ago, I worked at a sewing machine company. One day, I became ill at work and had to leave early. I just felt horrible, like the sudden onset of a really bad cold. Since any kind of cold meant serious trouble for me, I called my doctor, who actually came out and made a house call. He diagnosed pneumonia and prescribed antibiotics, remarking that it was a miracle I could still breathe at all.

Later, I learned that the doctor had told my husband I'd probably die, and that he should start making arrangements for the funeral. Doyle didn't let on, though, because he didn't want me to be frightened.

Doyle insisted on a second opinion, and my doctor referred me to a specialist in respiratory medicine. This doctor hospitalized me immediately and began a battery of tests. It was then that we learned that despite the tubal ligation I was pregnant, about three months along, and that the pregnancy was the cause of my latest respiratory difficulties. The doctors were very worried and said that the pregnancy was life threatening. If I tried to carry a child to term, they told me, I would probably not survive and neither would the baby. They advised me to have an abortion.

Doyle and I were well aware of the risks, yet we were also thrilled at the prospect of bringing a new life into the world. But we're realistic too, and we knew that even if I was able to take the pregnancy to term, there was a high probability that both the baby and I would die.

Irene and Doyle decided that an abortion was their only choice. At first Irene worried that the loss of their unborn child might weaken her relationship with Doyle, but the crisis seemed only to strengthen it further.

I've been very fortunate to be married to a terrific man whose patience and understanding of my disability make living life on a respirator a whole lot easier. Doyle and I have a solid overall relationship. And he is even able to make our sex life much more pleasurable for me than I would have ever thought possible.

I had little sexual experience before I met Doyle. When we married, he guided me through the sexual learning process with tenderness, sweetness, and a forgiving attitude toward my sexual shortcomings. Because of my respiratory problems, I find it especially difficult to breathe when we're making love. The usual gasps and pants of ecstasy are not what they seem to be. Unless I'm really into sex, really excited, that loud breathing is actually me fighting for air.

I have to admit I don't crave sex often, mainly because of my respiratory troubles. I guess I'm afraid of not being able to breathe at all. Doyle's very understanding about this and goes to great lengths to get me very aroused and turned on. Without his patience, sex would probably not be very pleasurable for me. But Doyle knows exactly what to do, and, when I get really excited, I find it's easy to climax. It seems like I'm able to forget all about the breathing troubles once we both get carried away.

Other neuromuscular conditions present their own sets of problems. These include many lesser known disorders, such as dystonia, Huntington's chorea, and syringomyelia. Because these disabilities often do not get widespread public attention, they receive relatively little financial support. We hope that greater emphasis will be placed on these rarer disabling conditions during the next decade and that the organizations that serve men and women who have them will receive a greater proportion of funding—something that is long overdue.

Additional information on muscular dystrophy and other neuromuscular diseases is available through the following organizations:

Dystonia Medical Research Foundation
8383 Wilshire Boulevard, Suite 800
Los Angeles, CA 90211
(213) 852-1630

Cystic Fibrosis Foundation
6931 Arlington Road, No. 200
Bethesda, MD 20814
(301) 951-4422

Muscular Dystrophy Association of America
810 Seventh Avenue
New York, NY 10019

(212) 586-0808

National Genetics Foundation
P.O. Box 1374
New York, NY 10101

Chapter 14

CEREBRAL PALSY AND OTHER SPASTIC DISABILITIES

Cerebral palsy (CP) is a group of medical conditions characterized by nerve and muscle dysfunction resulting from damage to the part of the brain which controls and coordinates muscular action. According to the location of the damage, varying disabilities can occur. The most common effects are lack of muscle coordination and involuntary tremors, and there is sometimes difficulty with speech. Defective development of brain cells before birth, injury during delivery, an accident or infectious disease may all result in CP. The effects are permanent, and regular treatment is often necessary to prevent some of the resulting conditions from becoming more severe.

People with spastic disabilities are unable to fully control their movements because the muscles receive the brain's messages improperly. The result is that the muscles respond to normal stimuli by contracting instead of relaxing. As an example, a person with a spastic disorder may try to spoon cereal from a bowl up to his mouth. The brain transmits a message to the muscles, but the nervous impulse tells the muscles to contract instead of relax, or to relax instead of contract. Or the muscle may attempt to contract and relax at the same time. The result is jerky, abrupt movements over which the person has little or no control.

The degree of disability caused by CP varies greatly. In some people, it may only affect certain muscle groups, and the degree of spasticity can range from barely perceptible to extremely severe. Cerebral Palsy also frequently affects speech because of lack of coordination of the vocal muscles. The result is sometimes garbled speech that can be very hard to understand, especially for those unaccustomed to hearing it. In some individuals with CP, a speech dysfunction may be barely noticeable. In others, speech may be so labored as to be incomprehensible.

When people with cerebral palsy have had extensive brain damage, there may also be some degree of mental disability. Again, as with CP's other manifestations, this can range from a mild learning disability to severe mental retardation. More typically, people with cerebral palsy have perfectly normal mental abilities. In fact, more often than not, people with cerebral palsy are highly intelligent.

Cerebral palsy also does not produce any changes in tactile sensitivity. People with CP have complete sensory ability, and they feel the same things anyone without the disorder might feel. These include responses to sexual stimuli and physical desire.

Some people with cerebral palsy may have difficulty expressing themselves sexually because of the severity of their spasticity. The contractions of severe muscle spasms, for example, may make it impossible for a woman with cerebral palsy to

open her legs to give a man enough access to enter her vagina. One solution might be to use the various rear-entry positions, which allow intercourse while the woman's legs remain closed.

For a man with severe contractions in the legs and hips, it may be equally impossible to straighten his legs enough for his penis to enter the woman. This may limit the man to manual stimulation of his partner or of himself as a way of experiencing sexual pleasure.

Cerebral palsy imposes a wide variety of limitations, and most people with the condition usually have to approach sex creatively and adapt standard sexual positions and techniques to their individual needs and abilities. What works for one person may not work for another.

Rochelle has had cerebral palsy since birth. She was born two and a half months premature, after her mother sensed that her baby had suddenly stopped moving inside the womb. Rochelle's mother was hospitalized, and doctors performed an emergency cesarean section. But, despite how quickly the problem was detected, Rochelle spent her first three months clinging to life in an incubator to compensate for lost development time.

By that time Rochelle had suffered permanent brain damage which, although barely detectable at first, caused cerebral palsy. At the age other babies would have been laughing, crying, and starting to crawl, Rochelle seemed totally uninterested in her surroundings and was generally unresponsive. It took doctors more than a year to determine that her problem was CP and that it had been caused by lack of oxygen to the brain just before her premature birth.

Fortunately, the damage to Rochelle's brain was relatively minor, leaving her with a mild form of cerebral palsy that primarily affected her legs. It causes her to have an awkward gait, a noticeable limp, and difficulty with balance. Today walking is for her the result of deliberate, conscious effort. When the weather is cold and wet, Rochelle's legs become especially stiff and painful. She still falls down frequently and often needs assistance to walk on snow or ice.

Looking back, Rochelle remembers feeling equally awkward in her social development:

Ever since I can remember, my relationships with the opposite sex have been primarily platonic. Men seemed to think I was wonderful as a friend or buddy ... but nothing more. Then again, I always seemed to attract guys who had serious personality or social disorders. I guess they assumed I was more approachable because I was disabled. Due to my past experiences with personal rejection, I tended to be nice to these men, even the "oddballs." I could never be outright rude and tell them to leave me alone. Some of these guys would just latch onto me, and even follow me around. This was sometimes frightening, especially if they were clearly unstable. I wouldn't know exactly what their mental state was. It concerned me that I might be provoking someone who was actually dangerous. I became wary of men, and I began to think that anyone who wanted to approach me was a bit of a weirdo. Because of this, I started to reject most relationships even before they had begun.

This almost caused me to miss out on meeting the man I would eventually marry.

When I was younger, I assumed that I would not marry someone who also had a disability. It seemed unwise since I needed help myself at times and really wasn't able to care for the physical needs of another disabled person. This sounds funny, but it also struck me that it would also be a loss of status to marry a disabled man; it might look like I was "settling" for the only kind of man available to me. I know now that I was wrong in adopting that outlook, but that's how I felt at the time.

It's still amazing to me that, despite my attitudes, I fell for my husband, who is also disabled. He has a form of CP quite different from my own. We're able to complement each other physically; he helps me when I need it, and I help him. I find it a great relief not to have to keep up physically with the needs of a nondisabled person.

Although Rochelle's husband, Terry, is also disabled by cerebral palsy, his disability is much less visible. Terry's spasticity in his arms and trunk muscles is not evident except when he writes or uses other fine motor skills. Terry's CP is the result of a congenital defect that also left him with a moderately severe hearing impairment. To compensate, he relies heavily on lipreading. At times, Rochelle finds Terry's communication disability annoying:

> *Terry's hearing impairment is really bothersome for us when we argue or are genuinely upset. Then his lipreading goes all to hell; I forget to look at him when I talk, and he forgets to look at me. Generally, though, we get along quite well.*

> *As for romance, Terry and I, thank goodness, have a very satisfying sex life. We're both very sexual beings, and what our disabilities may prevent us from doing in quantity, we make up for with quality. The impaired flexibility of my legs means I may not be able to be as athletic in bed as another woman might. During intercourse, I usually have to change positions frequently, but it's really no big deal. I also notice that my legs tend to stiffen more as I become increasingly aroused, so we have to compensate for that. But, in fact, I feel very "undisabled" while having sex with Terry, and the disability really doesn't get in the way.*

> *I think it helps to have a lover who truly values my happiness and pleasure. Terry is wonderful about this. Both of us treat each other as sexual beings and are very creative and communicative about finding the best ways to enjoy mutual satisfaction.*

> *We are very happy and extremely good for one another. God has really blessed us.*

Sheryl is another woman disabled by cerebral palsy. She has severe spasticity in her arms and legs. Disability-related surgery and several accidents have left her unable to carry her own weight reliably, so she uses an electric wheelchair. She also has an attendant who helps with personal care, dressing, and transfering her in and out of the wheelchair. Sheryl's disability causes occasional bladder incontinence, about which she is very self-conscious. This has somewhat limited her social opportunities, although the limitation is partially self-imposed by her anxieties about possible odor or leakage.

An attractive woman now in her late twenties, Sheryl has a pleasant, outgoing personality and finds she makes friends easily. Throughout high school, however, she had few dates and even fewer serious involvements. She attributes much of this to her disability:

> Until I was about seven years old, I actually thought there was a disabled person in every family . . . that's how normal I thought I was. So I never really had problems in coming to terms with my disability; it was just there. It's only in recent years that injury and surgery have imposed further limits on my physical abilities. Accepting this is tougher. My mind still expects me to do some of the things my body no longer will.

> Socially, I find most able-bodied people consider me as a best friend or runner-up. I don't know how many times I've heard, "If only I wasn't in love with so-and-so, I'd be so interested in you." Yuck! I'll never be able to understand why so many AB's are incapable of seeing a disabled person as a potential lover. Do appearances really matter that much?

> The men I meet fail to realize that underneath this disabled body there lies a very sexy woman, one who is fully capable of friendship, love, companionship, and passion. My very existence centers around my female sexuality. It hurts when people try to suppress what I know is the real me.

> I went to college at a state university in the Midwest, located in a smallish rural community. For a school of its size, it had a large number of disabled students (because of the university's pioneering

program for disabled students). At the urging of the university's curators, the campus and the community surrounding it became extremely accessible to the disabled.

Ramps, special facilities, accessible housing—the whole nine yards—was right there for us to use. As a result, many disabled students stayed on in the community even after graduation. This kind of accessibility wasn't available in most other cities. So why leave? I've now been here eleven years.

When I began college, I was pretty close to a large group of other students with disabilities. In the group I started with, we all made the romantic circuit with each other at least once, and, if it hadn't sparked anything, it was generally accepted that it probably never would. After a few years, most of us came to be like brothers and sisters, a close-knit "family" of sorts. Most of us were gimps; we shared the common denominator of disability. Even a few AB's were among our close group, most of them attendants, care providers, or other people with a real interest in us as people.

Most of my romantic interests were with disabled teammates involved in wheelchair athletics (basketball, track and field, et cetera) and people affiliated with other university-sponsored activities for the disabled. So we had many common interests and abilities—more or less—right from the beginning.

When Arnie and I met, it was a mixture of instant antagonism and competition. I was the new kid on the basketball team, and he was the star. I wanted to take his ego down a notch; he wanted to prove his machismo. It backfired on both of us. In the first game of the season, Arnie (trying to show me the real way to play) got really trounced! It was the first time I saw him with his guard down, and I tried to soothe his damaged ego. Bad move. From there on, it was all uphill.

After a while, though, we started seeing each other. We were so different, yet in so many ways we were very much the same. Arnie, too, had CP, but his excellence at sports helped him overcome many of his problems with it.

Before we moved in together, we had separate apartments. When Arnie and I planned to spend the night together, I would have my attendant prepare me for bed in my apartment. Then, after she left, I'd struggle back into my chair by myself and make my way over to Arnie's apartment. I'd crawl in bed with him and we'd make love. Then I'd reverse the process and return to my place before his attendant arrived the next morning. Arnie would laugh and tell me I wasn't fooling anyone but myself. Maybe so, but at least I felt like that ruse gave us some semblance of privacy.

What a fantastic sex life we had! The only problems caused by disability were problems with my hips that made it difficult to part my legs. Arnie had to adjust to this, and it was difficult for us at first. But his gentleness and understanding were a big help. We found that lengthening foreplay helped relax my spasticity and made sexual motions a lot easier for us both.

After I graduated, I got a job. But although I was not good as a "housewife," Arnie wanted me at home. So I quit and stayed home, except that I found myself bored silly. Seeing my unhappiness, Arnie would disappear from my life for a few weeks, then pop up again just as quickly. It was a roller coaster ride.

Then I was hospitalized 350 miles away for corrective surgery. Arnie sent flowers and gifts and called me every day. He even got his sister to drive him up for a visit. When I saw his face, he looked even sicker than I was. He grabbed me, kissed me, and cried as he told me how much he loved me. I think he was just really scared that he was going to lose me. And with me away, he finally realized how much he needed me.

When I returned home, Arnie was waiting. A few days later he surprised me with a candlelit dinner (prepared by his attendant) and asked me to marry him. Every day until I gave him an answer, *he sent roses. Eventually, I said yes.*

We kept our engagement from our families until we could map out a way to deal with the negative backlash we knew would result. We never really did tell them because, after the ring was actually on my finger, I started to get second thoughts about the possibility of marriage. I suggested we step back a bit and think the whole thing over. But Arnie interpreted this as rejection, and we ended our relationship for nearly two years, or maybe I should say Arnie did. All this time, I did all I could to convince him how much I loved him.

A short time later due to poor attendant care and stress, my health declined. On the recommendation of a doctor, I went temporarily into a nursing home to rest and recuperate. I felt like a failure, since I had been living on my own for several years. I don't think Arnie dealt with my limitations very well. He made me feel I had failed him, too. I kept telling him that when my strength and health returned, I would come back to him . . . if he would have me. I told him how much I loved him and needed him, and how I'd never leave him again.

We could work it out, I thought. And when I returned home, Arnie was there. We began living together again. For exactly a week, we were inseparable. Then my ex-roommate announced that she was in love and would soon be getting married—to Arnie! He and I talked about this, and, while he admitted it was true, he never once said he was in love with her. I'll always believe he was still confused about his feelings for me.

A few months later, Arnie died very suddenly. I never knew exactly what happened. All I knew was that he was gone, and with him all our dreams of love and happiness and a good life together. Since then, I've felt half dead myself.

Though severely disabled by CP, Arnie was the sexiest, most alive man I ever knew. He was a proud and stubborn man who was at

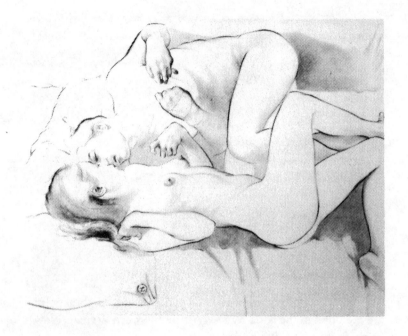

the same time a little boy full of mischief and mirth. He was passionate and unashamed about his body. And his tenderness awakened something in me I never knew existed. We shared the best and worst eight years of our lives, and I'm certain that each of us really loved the other every step of the way.

I miss him so much that I still can't put it into words . . .

Additional information on cerebral palsy and other spastic disorders is available through the following organizations and resources:

Association for Persons with Severe Handicaps (TASH)
7010 Roosevelt Way, NE
Seattle, WA 98115
(206) 523-8446

National Easter Seal Society
70 East Lake Street
Chicago, IL 60601
(312) 726-6200

United Cerebral Palsy Associations
7 Penn Plaza, Suite 804
New York, NY 10001
(212) 268-6655

Several powerfully written essays by people with cerebral palsy are included in the book *No Apologies,* by Florence Weiner (New York: St. Martin's Press, 1986).

Crusader is a magazine for people with cerebral palsy published ten times per year by the United Cerebral Palsy Associations.

Chapter 15

BLINDNESS AND OTHER VISION DISABILITIES

Blindness refers to any partial or total loss of vision. It is the inability to perform any work for which eyesight is essential. Blindness may result from injury to the eye itself or from some abnormality or lesion within the brain or the optic nerve. Or it may be caused by a systemic disorder, such as diabetes. Other causes include cataracts, detached retina, glaucoma, iritis, keratitis, ophthalmia, and various forms of trachoma. Some people are also born blind.

Like the majority of people with disabilities, those who are blind often encounter a lack of acceptance by society. Many people, it seems, feel vulnerable when encountering someone with blindness, perhaps because of deep-rooted fears about suddenly finding themselves in a similar situation. This often makes finding relationships difficult, although it is by no means impossible for people who are blind.

When George, age 50, became blind in his thirties, he was bombarded by well-meaning advice from friends and relatives:

Soon after I became blind, everyone started to encourage me to find a "nice little blind girl" who would be a good match for me. I knew they were trying to be helpful, but I really didn't care for the idea. It seemed to me that if anything ever developed where we'd make a relationship permanent, it would sure be nice to have someone around the house who could read the mail!

During college and for several years after, George had trouble finding the kind of romantic relationships he wanted.

For the most part, the women I was interested in tended to shy away from me. I'm reasonably sure it was due to anxiety over my blindness. It was clear they did not want to offend me, but they ended up being so overly nice to me that it was almost to the point of being patronizing.

Another problem I had, especially in my first few years of blindness, was in picking up on nonverbal and highly visual types of communication. Much of communication among people who aren't blind is done in nonspoken ways. Body language, postures, and facial expressions all have a lot to do with the way people communicate. As a blind man, I now had to learn how to pick up on these signals without seeing them.

It seems to be very difficult for most sighted women to be able to relate to a blind man as a romantic partner. Even after a woman has gotten to know me quite well, after she's become accustomed to my disability and its implications, there's always the possibility that the myths and prejudices of the sighted world may move in to put a damper on our relationship. This happened to me several times. I'd be deeply involved with a woman, and we'd be in a committed relationship, and then suddenly her friends or family would get increasingly scared and start tearing at the relationship. Suddenly, my formerly happy lover would become unsure about being involved with me, and the relationship would soon go sour.

I'd tell her, "Look, if I can handle it, you can too. Doesn't it mean anything that we love each other?" But it wouldn't do any good. The relationship would be over. Each time that happened, it would leave me feeling very depressed and extremely bitter. But, eventually, time has a way of healing all wounds. So after a while I'd move on to what I'd hope would be a better relationship.

I met one woman on the way to the bus stop after work one evening. I guess you could say we sort of bumped into one another. Literally! She accidentally stepped in front of me as I was walking down the street. I tripped and fell into a hedge, white cane and all. She helped me up, apologizing profusely and asking how she could ever make up for her clumsiness. I replied by saying she could go out to dinner with me. She laughed, agreed, and we dated several times.

Then there was another relationship where the woman's parents showed up at my apartment and accused me of being a hippie cult leader like Charles Manson. They said I must have their daughter on drugs, because why else would she be dating a blind guy! Their compassion and understanding were truly overwhelming. Needless to say, it didn't take long before the relationship ended.

After college, George began working as a rehabilitation counselor for a state agency. It was through his work that he met Marcia, a salesperson for a company that supplied services for the disabled. Their mutual attraction developed into love and eventually into marriage. They now have two teenage children.

Marcia and I had been dating for about three months before I met her parents. Previous to my first meeting them at Christmas, Marcia had only mentioned me to them in a phone call. Apparently the connection had been poor, and they had trouble understanding what Marcia had been saying about me. Her mom had apparently misunderstood her description of me, because as I stood on their front porch shaking their hands, I heard Marcia say, "No he's not black, he's blind." To which her mother replied, "Blind? Oh, thank God!" I don't agree with their bigotry, but I thought the whole thing was pretty hilarious.

Some sighted people contemplating relationships with a man or woman who is blind may be concerned about potential sexual incompatibilities. That may well be because, to most sighted people, the visual aspects of sexual expression play such an important role in becoming aroused. It is difficult to imagine making love without being able to actually see what's going on.

Jack, a man who was born blind as a result of complications from premature delivery, says sight isn't a prerequisite for sexual satisfaction and describes lovemaking as a "feast for the senses.

> *During lovemaking, my other senses—touch, smell, hearing, and taste—serve as the primary way I become aroused. The caress of my partner, and the way she touches me, is tremendously exciting, perhaps even more so than for a sighted person. The feel of her breasts on my face, the hardness of her nipples pressing into my palms, the brush of her hair across my chest, the lightness of her fingernails as she runs them up and down my body—these are just some of the ways I experience the incredible pleasures of sex.*

> *There was one sighted woman who knew exactly how to please me. She made our lovemaking even more stimulating by describing the way she looked and the sensuous atmosphere of the room. Then she would do this delicious striptease, slowly disrobing and carefully explaining what she was doing, what she looked like, and how she felt. At the same time, she would encourage me to use my hands and my mouth to stimulate her, to taste her naked skin and to skim over the few articles of clothing that she still had on. Finally, I would gently remove the final pieces of clothing, and we would make love all night.*

Other things I particularly enjoy during sex involve my other senses—especially smell, taste, and hearing. The bed lightly sprayed with perfume. The taste of freshly showered skin combined with the odors of sexual arousal and perspiration. The sounds of my lover's moans as her passion mounts. I get especially aroused by the sounds of my penis meeting the resistance of her vaginal lips and the raggedness of her breathing as it gradually increases until the final tightening and release. I am not really sure if any of those experiences are fully appreciated by the sighted, but I definitely enjoy them.

There are more than a million blind or visually disabled people in the United States today, of whom fewer than 50,000 are completely unable to see. Although increasingly visible in society and in the disabilities rights movement, people with blindness say that attitudinal barriers remain the most significant roadblock to their enjoying a successful and fulfilling life. In *Blindness: What It Is, What It Does, and How to Live with It,* Reverend Thomas J. Carroll explores those prejudices in depth:

We are afraid of all the effects of blindness: of the loss of reality contact, of being cut off from people, of the loss of our jobs, of financial insecurity and of loss of our normal mode of adjustment to living. We are afraid of ourselves and our weaknesses. We fear immobility and we fear dependence. Above all, we fear mutilation and the unknown. And we hate to face or admit our fears. In consequence, we (or at least the great majority of sighted people) will not look at our own attitude to blindness, nor will we look at blindness rationally. Many of us approach blindness and blind persons with our reason so hampered by conflicting emotions that it is almost impossible for it to function.

We hope that society will increasingly face these fears about blindness and address them honestly so that long-standing patterns of negative behavior toward people with all types of disabilities can be permanently relegated to the past.

Additional information on blindness and other vision disabilities is available through the following organizations and resources:

American Council of the Blind
1010 Vermont Avenue, NW, Suite 1100
Washington, DC 20005
(202) 393-3666

American Foundation for the Blind
15 West Sixteenth Street
New York, NY 10011
(212) 620-2000

Library of Congress
Division for the Blind and Physically Handicapped
1291 Taylor Street, NW
Washington, DC 20542
(202) 707-5100

National Association for Visually Handicapped
22 West Twenty-first Street
New York, NY 10010
(212) 889-3141

National Federation of the Blind
1800 Johnson Street
Baltimore, MD 21230
(703) 548-1885

Seeing Eye Dogs
Washington Valley Road
Morristown, NJ 07960
(201) 539-4425

Vision Foundation
818 Mount Auburn Street
Watertown, MA 02172

(617) 926-4232

How Do You Kiss a Blind Girl? by Sally Wagner (Springfield, Ill.: Charles C. Thomas, Publisher) 1986. This book shares the author's experiences as a person with blindness and offers suggestions for how people with visual impairments can enjoy romantic relationships. It also candidly discusses how blindness affects intimacy and provides pertinent advice for both people with blindness and sighted people with blind partners.

If You Could See What I Hear, by Derek Gill with Tom Sullivan (New York: Harper & Row, 1975). The story of a blind Boston folksinger who refuses to accept his blindness, this book was made into a popular movie in the 1970s.

Chapter 16

DEAFNESS AND OTHER HEARING IMPAIRMENTS

*P*erhaps more than any other disability, deafness cuts an individual off from the rest of society and imposes a double burden of isolation and loneliness. In a world of sound, the abilities to hear and speak normally are considered fundamental to human interactions. Those without hearing find themselves outsiders in this world. They are usually not only treated as invisible but viewed as too far removed from the mainstream to be full participants.

In fact, this is not the case. People with hearing and speech disorders generally spend more time and energy doing battle with public perceptions than they do with the day-to-day realities of their disability. There are more than 2 million people in the United States who cannot hear or speak and another 11 million who have some type of severe hearing impairment.

Deafness technically refers to a total or partial loss of hearing and has two types. In conductive deafness, a blockage or other problem interferes with the passage of sound to the inner ear; in perceptive deafness, there is damage or defective development of the inner ear, which is the actual organ of hearing. The degree of deafness depends on the type and extent of the condition, the age at which deafness began, and the training the person subsequently receives. Someone who is born deaf and therefore has never heard speech is usually at a greater disadvantage than someone who becomes deaf after learning to speak and read.

The terms *deaf-mute* and *deaf and dumb*, in addition to being completely demeaning to people who are deaf, are totally inaccurate. Most people who are deaf have nothing wrong with their vocal cords. They cannot speak, or are unable to speak clearly, simply because they cannot hear.

Deafness usually causes at least some degree of speech disability. This may range from a mild slurring of speech to total inability to form words and sounds. The ability to speak is a learned process which is almost totally dependent on a person's proficiency at imitating the speech of others. Unfortunately, deafness affects this ability and creates significant speech problems.

Deafness can be caused by a large number of diseases and disorders. Most commonly the cause is a disorder of the inner ear, the auditory nerve, cerebral pathways, or the auditory center in the brain. In many instances, the exact cause of deafness cannot be determined, even after extensive medical testing. Although some people are born deaf, deafness usually becomes noticeable gradually, with a slowly increasing loss of hearing.

Many people who are deaf use sign language, although the number of hearing people who sign is very limited. In situations where one is available, a deaf person may choose to rely on an interpreter.

Of course, interpreters are not always available, leaving the person who is deaf to his or her own devices. Some people who are deaf can be trained to lip-read. Though by no means a panacea, lipreading can help many people with deafness interpret the speech of the hearing world. Reading lips is difficult, however, and it requires that the speaking person always be looking directly at the person who is deaf. If the speaking person turns away, even for a moment, comprehension ceases.

Few people realize that even good lip-readers pick up on only 30 to 40 percent of spoken language. And if the person speaking has a lisp, stutter, or accent, this can reduce comprehension even further.

Some people who are deaf are able to produce speech even though they cannot hear themselves talk. This speech is sometimes quite distorted and difficult to understand. It may take several years of intensive speech therapy to produce speech that is readily understood, and many deaf people are unable to master this skill.

Because people with deafness often face multiple communications problems, hearing people are amazed that most deaf individuals are able to function well in today's world. But the majority of people who are deaf function by adapting themselves to their surroundings and compensating for their disability.

Although regular telephone communication is impossible for those who are deaf, many deaf people have a teletypewriter (TTY) connected to the telephone. This device enables a person to communicate directly with anyone else who has a TTY, including police and fire departments. Additionally, many areas have a telecommunications center called CONTACT, which enables people who are deaf to communicate over the telephone with hearing people. In this service, a hearing person serves as a go-between.

People who are deaf can, of course, read newspapers and other printed matter to keep up on current events. And they can watch television for news and entertainment. Many stations now offer closed-captioned viewing for the hearing impaired. This involves the attachment of a small decoder box to the TV set, allowing captions to appear on the bottom of the screen as the programs air. The effect is much like seeing subtitles for a foreign film. Most local cable companies provide decoder boxes free or at a nominal charge. Many people who are deaf can watch uncaptioned television, especially if they are able to lip-read.

Increased acuity of the other senses—sight, smell, taste, and touch—often permits a person with deafness to compensate at least partially for his or her hearing disability. Vigilance is the key: watching the food when it is cooking to be sure it doesn't burn, checking the baby to be sure he or she is not crying, and turning the sound level down on the television to be sure it's not blasting and annoying the neighbors. The list of tasks requiring hearing, and ways to compensate for a hearing loss, is seemingly endless.

Probably the most disabling characteristic of deafness is the restrictions it generally places on social contact. Because people with deafness can usually only communicate through sign language, many find themselves limited to a circle of acquaintances who are also deaf. Their hearing friends are those who can use sign. Romantic relationships for deaf individuals are nearly always with other people who are deaf or hearing people able to communicate in sign language. Many married people who are deaf also have deaf spouses. In fact, most dating experiences among people with deafness take place within the deaf world.

Hearing people tend to steer away from those who are deaf because it's very difficult to carry on a conversation with a person whose communications method is completely different from their own. When a hearing person tries to talk with someone who is deaf, it can be very frustrating for both. It's quite similar to conversing with someone who speaks a foreign language. Deafness limits communication to gestures, body language, and facial expressions. If either person gets even a smattering of insight into what the other has been trying to say, it's either coincidental or miraculous.

It's a sad fact that deafness may cause some relationships to end before their time. That's what happened to Noreen, a 40-year-old woman who has been totally deaf for the last eight years.

Noreen's deafness began at the age of eight, when she started to have difficulty hearing her teacher. A screening test indicated moderate hearing deficiency in both ears. Despite treatment by several doctors, Noreen's hearing continued to worsen. By the age of ten, she was fitted with hearing aids, but even these didn't seem to help much.

As she approached age 30, Noreen's limited hearing began to decrease even further. Over a three-year period, she noticed that fewer and fewer sounds were discernible, even when her hearing aids were tuned to their highest level of sensitivity. By the time she was 31, she was completely deaf in both ears.

Though hearing impaired most of her life, Noreen has been able to speak and communicate with others. She had a relatively happy childhood and adolescence, and had few adjustment problems in adulthood. After graduating from college, she married a hearing man:

> *I married the man of my dreams, a great guy who had accepted my problem of having a partial hearing impairment very well. At that time, I used a hearing aid and spoke perfectly. But when my hearing impairment progressed to total deafness, he told me he couldn't handle it. It really bugged him that I was unable to hear him when he spoke to me.*

> *I was having a hard enough time adjusting to not being able to hear. My husband didn't make it any easier. He'd shout at me all the time when I didn't respond to his words. We argued constantly for several months. Then, one day, he announced he was leaving.*

We got a divorce a few months later.

After that, Noreen was left alone in a silent world. It is not surprising that her husband's rejection hampered her adjustment, and she became very embittered about her circumstances.

She did have one factor strongly in her favor, however. Noreen had become deaf after her speech patterns had been established. After entering a training program for the deaf, Noreen learned to lip-read. Although she never became highly proficient at lipreading, she was able to use it to forge a new communications link to the hearing world.

Once this difficult period of her life was over, Noreen began actively to seek out new relationships. She is a gregarious individual who likes others and enjoys having many friends. But finding the right man proved difficult. Men were attracted to her, but it seemed that once the reality of her deafness sunk in, their interest faded.

Hearing men who are interested in me become wary about the possibility of a long-term relationship as soon as they notice my deafness. Usually it doesn't take long. We can be having a nice conversation, but, since I'm lip-reading, I lose the meaning of his words as soon as he turns his head. So I have to stop and ask him to look at me while he talks. This brings up all sorts of questions about my deafness and usually puts a real damper on things.

Hearing men seem not to want to be bothered with learning to speak my language. Learning to sign would seem to be a novel way of building a new relationship, but most hearing men seem unwilling to exert the effort. And signing is not tremendously difficult to learn (if the motivation is there, I suppose). I guess the relationship isn't meaningful enough at that point to generate the necessary motivation. It's their loss, I guess. But it's mine, too.

Although Noreen has had a difficult time finding romantic partners, she has been in several relationships since her divorce. Many of these have been long-term affairs that included sexual intimacy. Noreen has always been very proud of her sexuality. Being deaf has never affected her sexual desire in any way.

Noreen says that her most satisfying sexual affairs have been with deaf men:

> For the most part, I've dated men who are deaf. We have a much easier time communicating, and, as a couple, I can also use my speech and lipreading to serve as an interpreter and be a link to the hearing world.

> Hearing men just don't understand deafness. And it follows them to bed. I notice that my ability to lip-read goes right out the window as I get more and more excited. Lipreading requires intense concentration. During sex I have more important things to concentrate on. I still talk to my partner, but I really don't get any verbal feedback. Most guys don't do much talking anyway.

> So having sex is a silent thing for me. I've learned that the visual aspects of sex can more than make up for whatever there might be that I've missed due to my hearing impairment. You don't have to hear the sounds of sex to enjoy what you're doing. The sights, touches, aromas, and tastes are more than enough.

> The deaf men I've slept with have, in comparison, been much better lovers than hearing men. Deaf men seem to have the compassion when making love that lets you know they appreciate you more as a woman because you're more at ease with their deafness. They know you can't hear and realize what this means to you. They use more tactile stimulation, and in more and better ways than do hearing men. They concentrate on you, not just on the act of sex.

> Hearing men, on the other hand, tend to be vocal lovers, always talking and asking questions. Which does me no good whatsoever. What I need during sex is tenderness in the form of tactile love. And this should be accompanied by expressive use of body language and meaningful facial expressions. A hearing man, if he truly loves me, will make the effort to learn at least some signing that can be

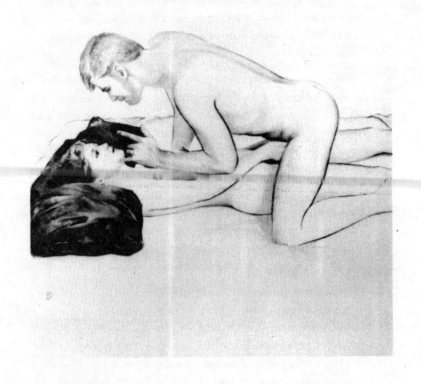

used in the bedroom. "I love you" is a simple sign that can be used quickly, even during sex. To see it on his hand while we are having intercourse would say to me that not only does he want me . . . but he cares.

Noreen has many friends who are also deaf. She belongs to several organizations for deaf people and devotes part of her spare time to an advocacy program for people with hearing disabilities. In this "second world" of deafness, Noreen is completely at ease, as are most of her friends. Together, they have no disability. They speak in sign and communicate daily over the TTY. It is only when they attempt to interact with those who can hear that their disabilities become noticeable. And, much like people with other disabilities, they find that nondisabled people remain aloof out of fear and uncertainty.

As Noreen puts it,

This may be a selfish idea, but it often struck me that it would be so much easier if no one had hearing, and we all talked in Sign. But, then, I guess that wouldn't be quite fair for those of us who are blind!

Neurologist Oliver Sacks, who wrote *The Man Who Mistook His Wife for a Hat*, theorizes in his book *Seeing Voices: A Journey into the World of the Deaf*, that the deaf think differently and may be more linguistically sophisticated than hearing people. Sacks calls deafness "a new form of visual intelligence."

"My feeling," Sacks says, "and it is only a hunch—is that there are some things that lend themselves more to signing and some things that lend themselves more to English. For example, English, being more abstract and linear, is more effective for metaphor and intellectual inquiry, while Sign, being more iconic and spatial, is better at conveying context and emotion."

Additional information on deafness and other hearing impairments is available through the following organizations and resources:

Sign Communication Department
Gallaudet University
800 Florida Avenue, NE
Washington, DC 20002
(202) 651-5200 202-651-5100 (TTY)

For information about sign language, sign language classes,
textbooks, and interpreting for deaf people.

Alexander Graham Bell Association for the Deaf
3417 Volta Place, NW
Washington, DC 20007
(202) 337-5220

American Humane Association/Hearing Dogs Program
P.O. Box 1266
Denver, CO 80201
(303) 287-3277

The Better Hearing Institute
Box 1840
Washington, DC 20013
(703) 642-0580

National Association for Hearing and Speech Action
10801 Rockville Pike
Rockville, MD 20850
(301) 897-8682

National Association for the Deaf-Blind
2703 Forest Oak Circle
Norman, OK 73071

National Association of the Deaf
814 Thayer Avenue
Silver Spring, MD 20910
(301) 587-1788

A Loss for Words: The Story of Deafness in a Family, by Lou Ann Walker (New York: Harper & Row, 1986). This moving autobiography describes how parental deafness affects hearing children.

Chapter 17

AMPUTATION

$\mathcal{M}$issing one or more limbs may be more than "just a little inconvenience," despite the title of a made-for-TV movie about the subject, but in most cases this disability does not have to prevent someone from enjoying every aspect of life. Nevertheless, amputation can limit mobility and require the use of prosthetics or adaptive techniques to perform many everyday activities.

Amputation, the complete surgical removal of any limb or any part of a limb, can be made necessary by many causes. Industrial and road accidents are the most common, but amputation may also be made necessary by diseases and conditions such as cancer, gangrene, frostbite, diabetes, and hardening of the arteries. Some amputees—such as the thalidomide babies of the 1950s—are born with missing limbs because of prenatal malformations or congenital defects.

Some amputees may even have more than one missing limb. It is not unusual for a person to have both legs missing, from an accident, or because of war injuries or birth defects. People with only one arm and one leg are less common, and those who have lost both arms even rarer. There are also some people who have had three limbs amputated; quadruple amputees are quite rare.

The closer the amputation is to the body, the more disabling it is. This is because each limb has three main joints, each of which is responsible for the performance of specific physical motions. If a person's foot is amputated below the ankle, he or she may still be able to use a simple foot prosthesis and flex the artificial foot. But if part of the leg is amputated below the knee (BK), the person loses the ability to flex the ankle and a much more complex prosthesis is needed. And if an amputation is performed above the knee (AK), the person also loses the knee joint, requiring an even more involved prosthetic device.

There are essentially two types of artificial limbs: functional and cosmetic. Modern biotechnology and prosthetics have combined in recent years to produce limb replacements that react almost like actual limbs. In some instances, it is possible for an amputee to be fitted with electromechanical devices capable of performing many natural movements. These ingenious prostheses are capable of picking up small coins, holding a knife and fork, and enabling a person without legs to walk, albeit fairly slowly. It should be noted that artificial limbs, no matter how well constructed, never function exactly like real arms and legs. They also require a great deal of practice to use and call for an extended period of adjustment.

Men and women who have undergone amputation suffer from the same myths and stereotypes that affect their otherwise disabled cohorts. People stop and stare, make strange comments, and often fail to engage in anything but the most superficial social contact. The majority of people are still uncomfortable with visible differences, and not having an arm or leg clearly makes someone different.

At age 44, Jay became an above-the-knee, bilateral (double-sided) amputee overnight. He credits his fairly rapid adjustment period to a key realization about himself:

I've found that other people's reactions to my being disabled were often a reflection of my attitude about being disabled. Once I became comfortable with the "new me," this seemed to put others around me at greater ease and gave me greater social opportunities.

I can't say it was all a picnic though. My first serious effort at a romantic relationship after losing my legs ended abruptly because of my disability. Through a mutual friend, I had met and begun dating a recently separated married woman. We had a couple of dinner dates and also went to a ball game together. Before this, I had been very reluctant to get involved romantically because I'd been unsure how a woman would react to my not having legs. After dating this woman several times, I was starting to get an improved feeling of my masculinity and self-worth. Then came a romantic candlelight dinner in her home. Despite the fact we discussed the situation beforehand, once we were in bed together, she was really repelled by how my stumps looked. She was actually in tears. This effectively ended our relationship and left me feeling that my worst fears were confirmed—that I was no longer okay as a romantic partner because of my disability. It was a long time before I was ready to test the waters again.

Then I met Anne at a meeting of a support group for amputees. Anne is a paraplegic due to a skiing accident; she has also had elective surgery to have both legs amputated at the hip because she had intractable pressure sores. So, like me, she has no legs.

Anne and I hit it off fairly well, and I took her phone number and called her for a date the following weekend. The rest, as they say, is history. We discovered we were compatible in lots of ways, and soon we were seeing each other exclusively. After a while we decided to live together, and we've been together now for several years. Although neither of us consciously set out to find a disabled mate, there's a lot to be said for a partner who understands firsthand how it feels to be disabled.

Our romance, of course, led to sexual intimacies. I was a novice about sex with a disability, even though I'd been married before my injury. So Anne and I set out to discover the beauty of disabled sex together. Having found a loving and creative partner, I discovered that sex after being disabled was just as good as sex before my disability. Being an amputee interferes with sexual pleasure only minimally; my leglessness does somewhat reduce my mobility in bed and makes it difficult to turn over.

We don't use any special positions, techniques, or devices. However, since Anne's a paraplegic with little feeling in the usual sexual areas of her body, we've found that there are, in addition to intercourse, many other sexual activities (both in and out of bed, and even in a wheelchair) that can contribute to a satisfying sex life. I think that most people—nondisabled as well as disabled— tend to put too much emphasis on copulation at the expense of touching, fondling, kissing, and hugging. I like who we are sexually, and I've learned a great deal about true intimacy.

Corey was born without a right leg, and her stump extends about eight inches from her hip.

Perhaps the most difficult part of my disability is finding romantic partners who aren't upset by a disfigurement. After all, I was born this way and can't really do much about it. I don't know why it's so difficult for some people to accept that. I've been in two romantic relationships that came to an abrupt end when the men discovered they could not handle seeing my stump. That this happened twice within a very short period left me asking myself, What's the big deal about having two legs? Is it really that crucial to life?

I don't have any difficulty at all enjoying sexual activities, except that certain positions are difficult with only one leg, especially if I have to be on top. About the biggest sex problem I have is figuring out where to put the darned prosthesis!

Like the other men and women throughout this book, amputees are people first, and people with physical differences second. Although at times the concerns of amputees may have been overlooked because of a greater emphasis on people with spinal cord injuries or neuromuscular diseases, amputees' efforts to be recognized as full human beings are beginning to take center stage as this group plays an increasing role in the disability rights movement.

Additional information on amputation and prosthetics is available through the following organizations and resources:

Amputees' Service Association
P.O. Box A3819
Chicago, IL 60690
312-583-3949

National Amputation Foundation
12–45 East 150th Street
Whitestone, NY 11357
(718) 767-0596

The One-Hander's Book: A Basic Guide to Activities of Daily Living, by Veronica Washam (New York: John Day, 1973). This is an illustrated guide to mastering daily activities for men and women who have use of only one hand.

Chapter 18

OTHER DISABLING CONDITIONS

*M*ost people with disabilities have conditions that are in some way apparent to the rest of society. Those with paralysis use wheelchairs or crutches, for instance. Individuals who are blind may rely on a cane or a guide dog. And deafness is usually noticeable when communication is taking place. But some people have disabling conditions that do not reveal themselves in external differences or in significant physical restrictions—yet these people clearly face many of the difficulties associated with being disabled in our society.

One example is a rare inherited, noncommunicable disease called *neurofibromatosis*, also known as "Elephant Man's Disease" because of the way it can alter the shape of someone's head. Englishman John Merrick, a figure during the Victorian period who had neurofibromatosis, was also known by this name, and he was later immortalized in a play with the same title. Neurofibromatosis causes widespread nonmalignant tumors of the peripheral nerves. The tumors lie slightly below the skin all over the body. Although the condition causes pain in its milder forms, it is generally tolerable and may not cause significant disability.

Neurofibromatosis produces a multitude of protruding skin tumors. Its manifestations are considered difficult to look at, so most of society finds it easier to shun people with this condition. They are treated as though they have a disability, even though their individual situation may not in itself be physically disabling.

As a person with neurofibromatosis, Mary has experienced firsthand its "disabling" effects. She inherited the disorder from her father, as did her younger sister. Mary's condition is much milder than that of her sister, who has so many tumors on her body that she is unable to walk or care for herself. Mary is perfectly capable of performing most physical tasks. She suffers only mild periodic discomfort when the inflammation flares up, and she has a slight hearing loss because of tumors inside her ears.

Mary says she tries hard not to react to the constant stares, whispers, and pointed fingers she endures whenever she's out in public. But tuning them out is extremely difficult.

Most of my limitations, I suppose, are psychologically imposed. I am able to do most things (some with a bit of discomfort), but because of my poor self-image and more bad experiences than I can count, I've had trouble finding and sustaining relationships. I was married for eight years and had two children. But since my divorce, with one exception, I've avoided meeting men and have turned down the few who have asked me out. I still find men attractive and would love to have a warm, close relationship with someone. But I'm so fearful of being continually found repulsive or ugly or just plain undesirable. I know I may be blowing things out of proportion, but it's difficult to get that constant fear out of my mind.

Initially, Mary felt her disability was responsible for the breakup of her marriage. In time, however, she realized it was her husband's perception of her that led to the demise of their relationship. His view of her was significantly affected by the opinions of others. What began as a loving relationship ended when their reactions became more important to him than Mary's worth as a human being.

When we first got married, he said he loved me for who I was on the inside, and the disorder didn't matter to him. That lasted about a year. Then, once he saw how others reacted to me over and over again—especially his male buddies—he didn't seem to be able to take it anymore. He began to imply he was having trouble finding me attractive or sexually appealing. At one point he even told our children (they were seven and eight years old) that I had an "ugly body." I'm glad the kids were too young to understand most of what was going on, but I knew that it was the beginning of the end for us. We divorced not long after that. It still surprises me how anyone could be that cruel. And he was an intelligent man who I thought was a sensitive person. I guess I was wrong.

The divorce affected me very deeply. Not only had my disability ended my marriage (or so I thought), but it also had a lot to do with other relationships I had later. For several years, I had no dates, and, actually, I'd nearly given up on ever finding anyone. Then I met Frank, a gentle, kind man with whom I had a close and intimate relationship for several months. We almost got married, but I found myself unable to cope with my insecurity about my appearance. I would not appear in front of Frank completely naked. Yet he wanted me to; he told me I should be proud of my body, since that was the way God had made it. There was nothing to be ashamed of, he said. Frank really loved me.

But I was too inhibited. We finally broke up. Frank just couldn't stand it that I was so uptight about my body. He assured me that all those bumps on my skin meant nothing to him. It was just the way I was, and he loved me, not my skin. Maybe I was afraid he'd turn out to be like my ex-husband; so I allowed our relationship to slide down the drain.

A few years ago, Mary entered therapy to help overcome her fears of rejection. The counseling, apparently, has been helpful; Mary is again looking for a new relationship. She has begun dating, and her new outlook has helped her become more accepting of herself.

Counseling has helped me a lot. I used to believe that my disability caused me not to be attractive to any man. I suppose I knew it wasn't true, but I had a hard time shaking that feeling. There is a man at work who has asked me out many times, but I've always turned him down. There were many reasons why I said no, but always in the background I felt ugly and unworthy of love and affection.

Realistically, I know that my condition is no worse than burn scars or chronic eczema. I've often wondered how those people handle it. Since entering therapy I've come to realize that I'm basically a good person who is fully capable of giving and receiving love. And I'm friendly, amusing, and easy to get along with. It's only recently, after years of telling myself I can't, that I've come to realize I can have normal relationships.

My parents raised me to believe that it's what's inside a person that means the most, and that a beautiful exterior doesn't make you desirable. What you are is more important than what you look like. Somewhere along the line, their teachings faded away in my mind, and that resulted in years of emotional pain.

I've begun to accept dates—from a guy at work and others—and now I think I have a better chance at finding a good relationship.

Eileen is another example of a person who does not have what is classically considered a disability but is stigmatized and condescended to because of physical differences. She has PSEUDOACHONDROPLASIA, one of almost a hundred types of dwarfism. The condition is thought to be hereditary, the result of a gene mutation, although the specific gene has not yet been identified.

Eileen stands approximately three feet eight inches tall and has arms and legs that appear disproportionate to the rest of her body. (Although the terms are mistakenly used interchangeably, a person with *dwarfism* should not be confused with a person who is a midget. A *midget* is an adult who, for one reason or another, has not achieved full growth. He or she has a perfectly proportioned body, just smaller than that of a full-grown adult. People with dwarfism have moderately developed bodies with shorter limbs.)

Although Eileen does experience the stiffness and tenderness in her weight-bearing joints that is common in dwarfism, her small stature does not really constitute a disability. Most of Eileen's limitations are imposed on her by society's negative reaction to her size.

My problems are mainly those created by having to deal with a society that expects everyone to be five feet or taller. Most physical structures are built to accommodate people of normal height. There is no regard given to "little people"—it's like we don't exist. For instance, I can walk into a store and stand at the counter waiting for a salesperson. If I don't speak up (loudly), no one will notice me, and, yet, if someone of normal height comes by, they'll be waited on immediately.

In addition, my dwarfism has caused some degenerative hip disease similar to arthritis. Walking long distances is painful at times and very tiring. With my short legs, I have to take three steps where a normal person would only take one; that means I have to use three times the energy to walk the same distance. Walking up and down stairs is also becoming difficult, more so as I've become older.

Though I've always had a lot of friends, finding romantic relation-ships has always been a problem. At times, it was difficult to deal with. I had no romances or dating relationships in high school, and very few in college. I think the general, nondisabled public does not see anyone with physical differences as desirable (especially in affluent areas, where "image" is everything).

In some instances, I think I actually contributed to my lack of romantic relationships. Although I wanted these kinds of loving relationships, the rejection I'd experienced caused me to develop the attitude that I'd probably never actually find anyone who'd accept me as I am. I think that I must have subliminally (and sometimes overtly) communicated this to potential partners. I was also very self-conscious and found it really difficult to relax around the men I liked. All this combines to be a great way to make men lose their interest.

What is especially frustrating for Eileen is that many people look on dwarfs as a source of humor. *Snow White and the Seven Dwarfs* did little to advance equality for the "little people," she feels; neither did *Alice in Wonderland* or all the other children's stories that depict dwarfs as happy-go-lucky clowns, objects of mirth, or evil trolls.

What I really have a hard time swallowing is the way the public always seems to think that people of small stature are happy little nobodies, just laughing their lives away without a care in the world. This "sideshow mentality" is what makes dwarfism a disability. They expect us to be either in the movies or in a freak show. When we're out in public, people laugh at us, stare at us, and make us the object of ridicule. If they only knew what a lousy life it is trying to live in their world when you're under four feet tall.

I've learned to put up with this invisible but clearly felt wall between me and others. And I don't let my guard down until I know or sense that the person I'm dealing with is "okay." Then if they ask questions it's because they're sincerely interested and not trying to be invasive.

Unfortunately, this also puts some people off. I may miss meeting some good people, and may be passing up some worthwhile relationships. But it's worth it to me if I don't have to put up with the constant comments and ridicule. Here I am, a successful career woman who operates a company with a staff of twenty people. Yet when I go out in public, I still have to listen to inane comments about how funny I look or how cute I am. It's no wonder I'm cautious about meeting people.

It had often occurred to Eileen that her best chance for finding romantic fulfillment might be with a man who was also a dwarf. But she always thought that if she became involved with a fellow dwarf, it would mean that she had "given up," that she was unable to attract anyone else.

Then she met Rick. They had known each other briefly at college, but she'd barely given him a second look because Rick was also a dwarf. Their conversation led to a lunch date the next day, and soon they were seeing each other regularly. Having a man in her life who really understood what it means to be less than four feet tall in a six-foot world was a new experience for Eileen, and she thoroughly enjoyed it.

Eileen and Rick fell in love and began an intimate relationship, adding an entirely new dimension to Eileen's life. Here, at last, she had found a way to express her long dormant sexuality with a man who really understood her needs, her capabilities, and her worth as a human being.

My relationship with Rick was my first truly romantic interaction with another person. He's the greatest guy in the whole world! Despite what looks back at me when I look in a mirror, Rick sees me as beautiful, sexy, and desirable. We're married now, but he's not just my husband; he's also my best friend. We can talk and be playful and be serious when we have to be. Rick accepts me as is. He encourages me to be who I want to be and to go after what I want in life. Ours is a very comfortable relationship with just the right amount of sizzle and attraction. We're really good for each other.

Even sex, which I knew practically nothing about until I met Rick, is fantastic. Before I met him, I knew I was a sexual person, yet I never knew how to express myself sexually. My sexuality was just there being stifled. I was afraid when the time came to have sex, I wouldn't be any good at it because I was a dwarf. How quickly I learned that dwarfism, or any other disability for that matter, has nothing at all to do with who you are sexually.

Dwarfs, incidentally, have sex just like anyone else. Just because one're "Little People" doesn't mean we don't make love in a big way. Except for a few minor adjustments to compensate for my joint stiffness, our sex life is wonderful. We've learned the importance of openness and communication, in our sex life especially, but also in everything else that has to do with our relationship.

There are also people who have "hidden" disabilities—physical differences that go unnoticed (at least for a time) by the rest of society. However, these are true disabilities, often necessitating major changes and adaptations in life-style. Some of the more common "hidden" disabilities are CARDIAC DISEASE, EPILEPSY, SPEECH DISORDERS, CHRONIC PAIN, some forms of ARTHRITIS, CANCER, EMPHYSEMA and other types of respiratory insufficiency, DIABETES, NEURITIS, ILEITIS, and COLITIS. Most people with these conditions do not appear to be disabled. Yet their "hidden" disabilities may have an impact on the success or failure of their social interactions.

Hidden disabilities can sometimes be extremely limiting. Tanya's disability is barely perceptible to those who do not know her. Yet she has been forced to retire early from her chosen career, because she could no longer keep up with the demands of her job and daily life.

Tanya has a rare inherited respiratory syndrome that results in severe allergic reactions to a wide variety of common airborne irritants. She is extremely allergic to cigarette smoke as well as to the odors of coffee, tea, and chocolate. Tanya's allergies also extend to many foods and medicines. She is virtually dependent on daily doses of cortisone and requires special nonallergenic insulin for diabetes.

Tanya is 27 years old, and her sensitivities first became apparent when she was in early grade school. They increased in severity over the years, to the point where she is now almost totally incapacitated by them. Tanya may look perfectly healthy, but those close to her realize the seriousness of her disability. She explains,

> *I cannot tolerate most common odors. A strong perfume or after-shave can set me off with severe bouts of asthma that leave me breathless and turning blue. I don't know how many times friends have called the paramedics for me when I had one of these attacks.*

> *Because of my allergies, I generally hide and try to avoid people. I try to worm my way out of most social encounters because about the only way I can prevent an attack is to load up on antihistamines and other drugs. My purse is like a pharmacy, with all kinds of prescriptions, antidotes, and nebulizers. I carry various injectables, including insulin for my diabetes, and many other drugs to have on hand just in case I need them.*

> *I also have to be very careful about infections. Even a common cold is a life-threatening condition for me. With me, there's no such thing as a case of the sniffles. Any strain on my respiratory system means I'll probably be hospitalized to prevent pneumonia. At times I've had to use a respirator when my lungs were overtaxed and weak.*

> *My opportunities for social contact are greatly limited by my disability. It's just not practical to ask everyone I meet to put on*

a surgical mask when they talk to me—people would think I was nuts! If I go out in public, I have to be careful to avoid any of the irritants that set off my asthmatic episodes. So I'm really very limited socially.

I still have my good days, where my strength is up, and I'm more resistant to all the things I'm allergic to. I have some friends over, and at times I do manage to get out to lunch, shop, or just spend a day with my friends. I found this one theater where it's nice to go to the movies. There's no smoking, the air conditioning always makes it comfortable, and, if I go in the afternoon, it's not very crowded and I don't have to worry as much about catching colds from people around me.

When I met Wayne, the severity of my allergies was not nearly what it is today. We've been married six years, quite happily I might add, and he's stuck by me through all the medical problems. Since I've become totally disabled, Wayne has tended to treat me like I'm delicate and have great needs that demand special priority. Sometimes he tends to overdo it. I appreciate his concern but would prefer less attention at times. Yet he loves me and is concerned for my welfare. I guess I'm pretty lucky.

Wayne and I share a good marriage. Every day I thank God for bringing this man into my life. I have nervously sweated it out through several severe illnesses and finally disability retirement, waiting for Wayne to show some sort of anger, disgust, or negative reaction. He has responded only with love, support, and stamina throughout the whole experience. He married a successful woman with a thriving career and a nice income. Now all of this has changed. But we're also closer and have acquired more marital and emotional strength by coping with my disability.

Tanya's disability also produces periodic episodes of chronic pain, particularly in her chest as she labors to breathe. The pain worsens on her "bad" days, when her strength ebbs. One would expect this to have a negative effect on Tanya and

Wayne's sex life, but, as Tanya says, it doesn't.

My respiratory difficulties at first seemed to really limit our sex life. Sex puts an increased demand on anyone's respiratory system, and I don't have the strength or stamina I want at least half of the time. And I can't control or predict when my periods of weakness will occur or how long they will last. You'd imagine that this would have destroyed the spontaneity of sex and, in most cases, it has.

I've found, though, that with careful planning it's still possible for us to have a satisfying sex life. Wayne and I use our creativity to develop positions, timing, and pacing so we can enjoy our sexual activity. When we have intercourse, I first have to get into a comfortable position with my chest elevated so I can breathe easier. We always place at least two pillows under my shoulders and make sure my head is not leaning backward (this would partially obstruct the airway, making it harder for me to breathe).

During intercourse, Wayne has to be careful not to jar my chest or in any way move, jostle, or rock my body. To those who are used to hot and heavy sex, with both people pounding away at each other, this seems pretty mundane. But, actually, it's not. Slow and easy intercourse can be just as pleasant. Maybe even more so, because the crescendo takes longer to build, and the sweetness of each moment is prolonged. Maybe everyone should try slow, careful sex once in a while; it's very satisfying. And if it's the only way you can have sex because of a disability, you appreciate it even more.

We usually don't have sex at all if I'm experiencing a lot of pain. Sometimes I have to take special medications or adjust my medication schedule so I can experience sexual activity. Some of my essential medications cause side effects that I have to prevent by taking other drugs. One of them (epinephrine) makes my head and extremities jittery and shoots my pulse up to 140 to 160 beats per minute; it takes about an hour for the effects to subside. But sometimes I need this drug to breathe better and to maintain the respiratory stamina demanded by sex.

My sex drive also vanishes when my blood sugar is low. This is especially annoying when we want to sleep late and make love in the morning (when my blood sugar is lowest). So I set the alarm for about dawn, take a couple of glucose tablets when it buzzes, and then go back to sleep. Then, when we're ready to make love, my blood sugar is up, and so is my desire.

To Wayne and me, sex is an episode of loving that also serves as a release from tension and a regenerating experience. We use sex as a rare and precious source of pleasure for a relationship often weary and worn down from illness, pain, and suffering. We create our own rules about sex, because no one else is us. And we're careful not to compare our sex life with those couples' in which both people have no disability. Our sex life is different, but not our sexuality. It is composed of elements that are unique to Wayne and me.

Sex can be the best medicine, and for me it is the best medicine. It lets me know I'm still alive.

Additional information on a variety of disabling conditions is available through the following organizations:

Dwarfism

Little People of America
7238 Piedmont
Dallas, TX
(214)388-4590

Epilepsy

Epilepsy Foundation of America
4351 Garden City Drive, Suite 406
Landover, MD 20785

(301) 459-3700

Ileitis and Colitis

National Foundation for Ileitis and Colitis
444 Park Avenue South, 11th Floor
New York, NY 10016
(212) 685-3440

United Ostomy Association
36 Executive Park, Suite 120
Irvine, CA 92714
(714) 660-8624

Spina Bifida

Spina Bifida Association of America
1700 Rockville Pike, Suite 540
Rockville, MD 20852
(800) 621-3141
(301) 770-7222

Strokes

Stroke Clubs of America
805 Twelfth Street
Galveston, TX 77550
(409) 762-1022

Various Disabilities

American Genetic Association
P.O. Box 39
Buckeytown, MD 21717
(301) 695-9292

Association for Persons with Severe Handicaps (TASH)
7010 Roosevelt Way, NE
Seattle, WA 98115
(206) 523-8446

Center for Independent Living
2539 Telegraph Avenue
Berkeley, CA 96704
(415) 841-4776

Disabled American Veterans
National Headquarters
P.O. Box 14301
Cincinnati, OH 45250-0301
(606) 441-7300

Gazette International Networking Institute (GINI)
4502 Maryland Avenue
Saint Louis, MO 63108
(314) 361-0475

Human Resources Center
201 I. U. Willets Road
Albertson, NY 11507
(516) 747-5400

National Association for the Physically Handicapped
2810 Terrace Road, SE
Washington, DC 20020

National Association of Protection and Advocacy Systems
220 I Street, NE, Suite 150
Washington, DC 20002-4362
(202) 546-8202

National Council on Independent Living
310 South Peoria Street, Suite 201
Chicago, IL 60607

(312) 226-5900

National Easter Seal Society
70 East Lake Street
Chicago, IL 60601
(312) 726-6200

The March of Dimes
1275 Mamaroneck Avenue
White Plains, NY 10605
(914) 428-7100

National Rehabilitation Association
633 South Washington Street
Alexandria, VA 22314
(703) 836-0850

National Rehabilitation Information Center
8455 Colesville Road, Suite 935
Silver Spring, MD 20910-3319
(800) 346-2742
(301) 588-9284

Office for Handicapped Individuals, U.S. Department of
Health and Human Services
200 Independence Avenue, SW
Washington, DC 20201
(202) 245-6568

Administration on Developmental Disabilities, U.S. Department of Health and Human Services
330 C Street, SW
Washington, DC 20201
(202) 245-2890

President's Committee on Employment of People with
Disabilities
P.O. Box 17413

Washington, DC 20041
(703) 471-5761

Rehabilitation International/
The International Society for Rehabilitation of the Disabled
25 East Twenty-first Street
New York, NY 10010
(212) 420-1500

United Way of America
701 North Fairfax Street
Alexandria, VA 22314
(703) 836-7100

Chapter 19

OUR HOPES FOR THE FUTURE

Despite the combination of joys and sorrows outlined in the preceding chapters, we remain optimistic about a brighter future and greater acceptance in every area of life for people with disabilities. But we also agree with Frank Bowe, author of *Comeback: Six Remarkable People Who Triumphed over Disability*. He believes certain characteristics will always be important if someone with a disability is to adjust successfully to his or her situation and find lasting happiness, whether alone or with a partner. These characteristics include:

DRIVE. Discipline, sheer hard work, and unremitting determination to succeed are needed by most people with disabilities who want to be successful in life and in work. This will, unfortunately, probably hold true for years to come, because surmounting barriers—whether they relate to physical factors, attitude, transportation, or communication—requires tremendous effort.

SENSE OF HUMOR. It's essential for a person with a disability to be able to laugh at himself or herself, at the ignorance of most people about disabilities, and at the world itself. The struggle to succeed is a long and hard one. Without humor, the oppression one faces will induce depression and hasten defeat.

PATIENCE. For many of the reasons just noted, a disabled person must develop a long-range view of life, accepting what cannot be changed and realizing that what can be altered will not change quickly.

EDUCATION. A solid regular education (as opposed to segregated special education) is necessary to provide a strong foundation for achievement and satisfaction in every area.

REHABILITATION. For many, if not most disabled people, further training, particularly in work-related areas, is necessary. Rehabilitation also includes counseling, provision of therapy, and other kinds of assistance.

SUPPORTIVE FRAMEWORK. Whether it be parents, teachers, friends, or loved ones, it's vital for the person with a disability to develop a support network that provides a sense of security and protection in an often unaccepting world.

CURIOSITY. Disability often means deprivation of an important source of information about the world. Deafness, for example, may deny a person reliable means of communication with other people. A physical disability often robs a person of the chance to learn about as many experiences as do other people. To go beyond these artificial boundaries requires will, which means developing and maintaining a healthy sense of curiosity.

INFORMATION ABOUT DISABILITY. People who are disabled often have difficulty identifying the precise effects of their conditions. Understanding his or her disability enables a person to separate strengths and weaknesses and to know what goals are realistic, at present and over the long term.

OUR HOPES FOR THE FUTURE

ACCESS TO TECHNOLOGY. Devices are available which can obliterate many of the problems associated with disability, and disabled people should try to obtain and use whatever technology can be helpful to them. There are machines that read along for people who are blind, devices that enable people who are deaf to use the telephone, electric and manual wheelchairs, automobile adaptive devices, vans, and other mobility equipment. These save incredible amounts of energy and time.

REALISTIC SENSE OF SELF. People with disabilities may have a very difficult time coming to understand themselves, judging themselves against others, and developing a sense of self-worth. Others may change the rules so a disabled person will "succeed" under reduced expectations; alternatively, others can be so hostile and harsh that they devastate the disabled person's self-concept. To become successful, the individual needs to know what his or her abilities and limits are. Plato's words still apply: Know thyself.

PRACTICAL AND SOCIAL INTELLIGENCE. The ability to deal with a variety of practical and social considerations helps shape and direct an individual's efforts to adapt and succeed. Drive without this kind of down-to-earth balance is wasted.

FRIENDLINESS. As stated in previous chapters, a disabled person who wants to be successful needs to be open to other people and to evidence toward them a sense of interest and welcome. He or she will need extra help at many crucial points; friendliness will get it, whereas antagonism discourages other from assisting.

Although the ideal is to prevent disabilities altogether, we believe now is the time for everyone to work together to make the world a more accepting place for people who do have disabilities. A vast gulf of understanding still stretches between the worlds of the disabled and the nondisabled. We must meet each other halfway across the bridge and make the remaining half far easier to travel.

Part Three

APPENDIXES

Appendix 1

HELPFUL SEXUALITY, FAMILY PLANNING, AND INDEPENDENT LIVING ORGANIZATIONS

Sexuality

American Association of Sex Educators, Counselors and
Therapists (AASECT)
435 North Michigan Avenue, Suite 1717
Chicago, IL 60611
(312) 644-0828

For a list of AASECT-certified counselors, send a stamped,
self-addressed envelope to this address.

Coalition on Sexuality and Disability
132 East Twenty-third Street
New York, NY 10010

(212) 242-3900

This nonprofit educational, advocacy, and networking organization works to assure the rights of people with disabilities to a full social and sexual life. In addition to publishing a newsletter, the group is a resource on interpersonal relationships, sexuality, social attitudes, and counseling.

> Sex Information and Education Counsel of the United States (SIECUS)
> 32 Washington Place
> New York, NY 10003
> (212) 673-3850

SIECUS is a clearinghouse for sexual education resources, referrals, bibliographies, and references as well as print materials and audiovisual programs. For more information, send a stamped, self-addressed envelope to this address.

> Sexuality and Disability Training Center
> Boston University Medical Center
> 88 East Newton Street
> Boston, MA 02118
> (617) 638-7358

This diverse group of psychologists, doctors, sexual health consultants, and others is a resource in New England for information on the relationship of physical disability and illness to human sexuality. In conjunction with Human Sciences Press, the center publishes the highly regarded *Sexuality and Disability Journal.*

> University of Michigan Sex and Disability Unit
> Department of Physical Medicine and Rehabilitation
> Box 33, Room E3254
> University Hospital

Ann Arbor, MI 48109
(313) 764-5335

Family Planning, Fertility, and Pregnancy

Planned Parenthood-NY
380 Second
New York, NY 10010
(212) 777-2002

Publishes the brochure "Contraceptive Services for Disabled People."

Independent Living Organizations

Planned Parenthood-SF
1660 Bush Street
San Francisco, CA 94109
(415) 441-7767

Publishes the brochures "Sex Education for Disabled People" and "Table Manners: A Guide to Pelvic Examinations for Women with Disabilities."

Dr. Larry Lipshultz
Baylor College of Medicine
Scurlock Tower
6560 Fannin, #1002
Houston, Texas 77030
(713) 798-4001

Walter Verduyn/Covenant Rehabilitation Center
Covenant Medical Center
2101 Kimball Avenue
Waterloo, Iowa 50702
(319) 292-2268

Specialists in conception and pregnancy for women with disabilities.

> Department of Family Services
> Craig Rehabilitation Hospital
> 3425 South Clarkson St.
> Englewood, Colorado 80110
> (303) 789-8000

> Dr. Bill Blank/Urology Department
> Huntingdon Reproductive Center
> 39 Congress Street
> Pasadena, California 91105
> (818) 440-9161

> Fertility Clinic
> National Rehabilitation Hospital
> 102 Irving St., NW
> Washington, DC 20010
> (202) 877-1620

> Dr. Carol Bennett/Urology Department
> Rancho Los Amigos Hospital
> 7601 East Imperial Highway
> Downey, California 90242
> (213) 940-7437

> George Szasz
> Shaughnessy Hospital
> 4500 Oak Street
> Vancouver, British Columbia V693M2
> (604) 875-2027

> Dr. Irvin Hirsch/Urology Department
> Thomas Jefferson Medical College
> Thomas Jefferson University Hospital
> Philadelphia, Pennsylvania 19107
> (215) 928-6961

Dr. Inder Perkash/Urology Department
VA Hospital-Palo Alto
3801 Miranda Avenue
Palo Alto, California 94304
(415) 858-3984

Independent Living Organizations

Association for Persons with Severe Handicaps (TASH)
7010 Roosevelt Way, NE
Seattle, WA 98115
(206) 523-8446

Center for Independent Living
2539 Telegraph Avenue
Berkeley, CA 96704
(415) 841-4776

National Council on Independent Living
310 South Peoria Street, Suite 201
Chicago, IL 60607
(312) 226-5900

National Rehabilitation Information Center
8455 Colesville Road, Suite 935
Silver Spring, MD 20910-3319
(800) 346-2742
(301) 588-9284

Appendix 2

DATING, FRIENDSHIP, AND
PEN PAL SERVICES

Handicap Introductions (HI!)
22 North Main Street
P.O. Box 232
Coopersburg, PA 18036
(215) 282-1577

This nationwide dating service for people with disabilities is
owned and operated by a psychologist.

PEOPLENET
Box 897
Levittown, NY 11756
(516) 579-4643

Robert Maura, a disabled man, founded this quarterly newsletter, which is designed so disabled and nondisabled men and women can meet other interesting people through a national network. For $15 per year, subscribers can place a fifty-word personals ad along with a photograph in the publication. In addition, *PEOPLENET* features well-written articles about dating, friendship, and sexuality.

Appendix 3

MAIL-ORDER INDEPENDENT
LIVING CATALOGS

Access with Ease
P.O. Box 1150
Chino Valley, AZ 86323
Cost: $1.00

This catalog carries products that can help make the life of a
person with a disability easier and more independent. Includes
a remote lighting system, reach extenders, and no-rinse shampoo and bath products.

adaptAbility
Department CH
Norwich Avenue
Colchester, CT 06415

(203) 537-3451
Cost: Free

This thirty-six-page catalog of innovative products for independent living is a boon to everyone from health-care professionals to consumers. About half the catalog is devoted to items for daily living, such as phone holders, doorknob adapters, jar openers, button hook/zipper pulls, portable shampoo trays, and bathtub rails, to name a few. adaptAbility is particularly strong on items for dressing and eating independently. The catalog also features clinical items, such as heat massagers, arm supports, and various types of cushions to prevent decubitus ulcers.

CLEO Living Aids
3957 Mayfield Road
Cleveland, OH 44121
(800) 321-0595
(216) 382-9700 (in Ohio)
Cost: Free

This catalog offers adaptive devices for use with sexual aids, such as spandex mitts.

Everest & Jennings Avenues
3233 East Mission Oaks Boulevard
Camarillo, CA 93012
(805) 388-7688
Cost: Free

This catalog carries clothing and accessories for wheelchair users in a variety of attractive fabrics and colors. Sample fabric swatches are even available.

Fred Sammons, Inc. Be OK!
Box 32
Brookfield, IL 60513
(800) 323-7305
(312) 971-0610 (in Illinois)

Cost: Free

This catalog offers a wide variety of independent living aids.

Frederick's of Hollywood
Box 229
Hollywood, CA 90099-0164
Cost: $3.00

Frederick's carries primarily lingerie, hosiery, and shoes.

Illustrated Directory of Handicapped Products
497 Cameron Way
Buffalo Grove, IL 60089
Cost: $14.95

This encyclopedic directory lists over seven hundred products to assist people with disabilities.

Mellow Mail
P.O. Box 8000
San Rafael, CA 94912
(612) 942-0388
Cost: $1.00

This catalog offers sexual aids, lingerie, books, and videos.

Synergist Erection System
Synergist Limited
6910 Fannin, Suite 304N
Houston, TX 77030
(800) 422-9005
(713) 796-9191 (in Texas)

This is a nonsurgical product for men with temporary or permanent impotence.

Twin Peaks Press (Disability Bookshop Catalog)
P.O. Box 129
Vancouver, WA 98666

(206) 694-2462

Helen Hecker publishes "The Disability Bookshop Catalog," a guide to 150 books on every aspect of disability, including relationships and sexuality. She is also the author of "Travel for the Disabled," "Wheelchair Vagabond," and the "Directory of Travel Agencies for the Disabled." Hecker heads the Traveling Nurse's Network, a service for people with disabilities who require a nurse for traveling.

Wings Convenient Clothing
Vocational Guidance Services
2239 East Fifty-fifth Street
Cleveland, OH 44103
(800) 227-6625
(216) 431-7800 (in Ohio)
Cost: $2.00

A catalog for women and men that features "easy wear—easy care" clothing with front and back Velcro closures. Includes skirts, blouses, and dresses for women and shirts and slacks for men. Wings also offers carry-all bags that affix to crutches or wheelchairs.

The Xandria Collection
Special Edition for Disabled People and Collector's Gold Edition
P.O. Box 317039
San Francisco, CA 94131
To order: (800) 242-2823
For customer service and information: (415) 952-7844
Cost: $4.00 for both

These catalogs offer sexual aids, vibrators, books, and lingerie. Include a note with your request for the catalogs stating that you are over age twenty-one.

Appendix 4

MAGAZINES, VIDEOS, AND COLUMNS

Accent on Living
Cheever Publishing
P.O. Box 700
Bloomington, IL 61702
(309) 378-2961
$8.00 per year

This is a dynamic, high-quality quarterly magazine exploring all aspects of independent living, including social and sexual relationships.

The Disability Rag
Advocado Press
Box 145

Louisville, KY 40201
(502) 459-5343
$12.00 per year

Now in its twelfth year, *The Rag* is probably one of the finest activist publications in the nation. It also offers a "best hits" collection of the most significant articles from previously published issues. The "Guide to Reporting on Disability" ($7.95) is required reading for any communications or journalism professional interested in writing about people with disabilities.

Independent Living and Health Care Today
Equal Opportunity Publications
44 Broadway
Greenlawn, NY 11740
(516) 261-8899
$15.00

This progressive health-care and life-style quarterly is one of the few disability magazines that regularly covers sexual issues. You'll find some fine writing here, including the insightful column "Sexuality and Disability" by activist Lorenzo Milam.

Kaleidoscope: The International Magazine of Literature, Fine Arts and Disability
Kaleidoscope Press
United Cerebral Palsy Foundation
326 Locust Street
Akron, OH 44302
(216) 762-9755
$9.00 per year

This is a semiannual literary and art magazine that effectively captures and reflects the experience of disability.

Mainstream: Magazine of the Able-Disabled
2973 Beech Street
San Diego, CA 92102

(619) 234-3138

Spinal Network Extra
Spinal Associates
P.O. Box 4162
Boulder, CO 80306
(800) 338-5412
$15.00 per year

This is an intelligent, caring publication aimed primarily at
people with spinal cord injuries. Spinal Network Extra is also
the home of the Spinal Network Bookstore, a terrific mail-order
resource for books on disability, including sexuality and relationships, women's issues, and medical topics.

> Sports 'n Spokes: The Magazine for Wheelchair Recrea-
> tion
> PVA Publications
> 5201 North Nineteenth Street, Suite 111
> Phoenix, AZ 85015-9986
> (602) 246-9426
> $9.00 per year
>
> Tell Them I'm a Mermaid
> VHS Video
> Available from Films Inc.
> 5547 North Ravenswood
> Chicago, IL 60640
> (312) 878-2600
> Cost: $79.00

This small gem by Vickie Ann-Lewis, an actress with a disability, brings together women with disabilities for a minimusi-
cal about their lives and loves. The title refers to the response
given by one of the women to annoying questions about her
physical appearance.

"Living with a Disability," a weekly syndicated column by Diane B. Piastro

This is the single best source of current information on every aspect of daily living for people with disabilities. Thoroughly researched, intelligently written, and incredibly helpful, this column is a must for anyone concerned with quality of life issues. If your local newspaper doesn't carry "Living with a Disability," write a letter to the managing editor suggesting it do so.

Bibliography

Accent on Living, Reprint Series No. 1 (selected articles on sexuality and people with disabilities). Bloomington, Ill.: Accent Press, 1974.

Bullard, David, and Knight, Susan. *Sexuality and Physical Disability: Personal Perspectives.* C.V. Mosby & Co., St. Louis, MO.: 1981.

Boston Women's Health Book Collective. *The New Our Bodies, Ourselves.* New York: Simon & Schuster, 1990.

Bowe, Frank. *Comeback: Six Remarkable People Who Triumphed over Disability.* New York: Harper & Row, 1981.

Bowe, Frank. *Handicapping America: Barriers to Disabled People.*

New York: Harper & Row, 1978.

Brecher, Edward, and the Editors of Consumer Reports Books. *Love, Sex and Aging: A Consumer's Union Report.* Boston: Little, Brown, 1984.

Butler, Robert, and Myrna Lewis. *Sex After Sixty: A Guide for Men and Women for the Later Years.* New York: Harper & Row, 1976.

Carroll, Thomas J. *Blindness: What It Is, What It Does, and How to Live with It* (Boston: Little, Brown, 1961.

Cassie, Dhyan. *So Who's Perfect!* Scottdale, Penn.: Herald Press, 1984.

Comfort, Alex. *The Joy of Sex.* New York: Pocket Books, 1987.

Comfort, Alex. *More Joy of Sex.* New York: Pocket Books, 1987.

Craig Rehabilitation Hospital. *Handbook on Sexuality After Spinal Cord Injury.* Englewood, Colo. Craig Rehabilitation Hospital, 1987.

Dodson, Betty. *Sex for One: The Joy of Selfloving.* New York: Harmony Books, 1987.

Duffy, Yvonne. *All Things Are Possible.* Ann Arbor, Mich. A. J. Garvin & Associates, 1981.

Fine, Michelle, and Adrienne Asch, eds., *Women with Disabilities: Essays in Psychology, Culture and Politics.* Philadelphia: Temple University Press, 1988.

Gallaudet University. *Social Aspects of Deafness: Vol. 5, Interpersonal Communication and Deaf People.* Washington, D.C.: Gallaudet University Press, 1983.

Gallaudet University. *Social Aspects of Deafness: Vol. 6, Deaf People and Social Change.* Washington, D.C.: Gallaudet University Press, 1983.

Gochros, Harvey and Jean, eds. *The Sexually Oppressed.* New York: Association Press, 1977.

Gregory, Martha Ferguson. *Sexual Adjustment: A Guide for the Spinal Cord Injured.* Bloomington, Ill.: Cheever Publishing, 1974.

Hale, Glorya, ed. *The Sourcebook for the Disabled.* New York: Paddington Press, 1979.

Heslinga, K., et al. *Not Made of Stone.* Springfield, Ill. Charles C. Thomas, 1974.

Higgins, Paul. *Outsiders in a Hearing World: A Sociology of Deafness.* Beverly Hills, Calif.: SAGE Publications, 1980.

Hopper, C. Edmund, and William Allen. *Sex Education for Physically Handicapped Youth.* Springfield, Ill.: Charles C. Thomas, 1980.

Kleinfield, Sonny. *The Hidden Minority: America's Handicapped.* Boston: Little, Brown, 1979.

Lovering, Robert. *Out of the Ordinary: A Digest on Disability.* Phoenix, Ariz.: ARCS, 1985.

McCarren, Marie. "Birth Control for Spinal Cord Injured Women." *Spinal Network,* Spring 1989, 41–43.

"Meet Ellen Stohl." *Playboy,* July 1987, 68–75.

Mooney, Thomas O., et al. Theodore M. Cole, and Richard A. Chilgren. *Sexual Options for Paraplegics and Quadriplegics.* Boston: Little, Brown, 1975.

Muilenburg, Alvin L., and A. Bennett Wilson, Jr. *A Manual for Above-Knee Amputees.* Houston, Tex. self-published, 1984.

National Information Center on Deafness. *Communicating with Deaf People.* Washington, D.C.: Gallaudet University Press, 1987.

Bibliography

Oakes, Ruth. "The Impact and Implications of Physical Disability in Women." Paper presented at the fifth annual meeting of the Society for Behavioral Medicine, Philadelphia, 1984.

Sacks, Oliver W. *Seeing Voices: A Journey into the World of the Deaf.* Berkeley: University of California Press, 1989.

Sandowski, Carol L. *Sexual Concerns When Illness or Disability Strikes.* Springfield, Ill. Charles C. Thomas, 1989.

Schover, Leslie R. *Sexuality and Cancer.* New York: American Cancer Society, 1988.

Task Force on Concerns of Physically Disabled Women. *Toward Intimacy: Family Planning and Sexuality Concerns of Physically Disabled Women.* New York: Human Sciences Press, 1978.

Smith, Jerd. "Making Babies: The Boom in Men's Fertility." *Spinal Network,* Spring 1989, 38–41.

Wagner, Sally. *How Do You Kiss a Blind Girl?* Springfield, Ill. Charles C. Thomas, 1986.

Weiner, Florence. *No Apologies: A Survival Guide and Handbook for the Disabled, Written by the Real Authorities—People with Disabilities and Their Families.* New York: St. Martin's Press, 1986.